OF MICE AND MOM

THE BEST OF THE INSIDER

2002-2010

BY: MICKEY SWITALSKI

TABLE OF CONTENTS

Youth Will Be Served

Sports

Policy

Budget Blues in the Red

Politics

Poetry

Introduction

As I sit here in Lansing, cleaning out my office as my Senate career draws to a close, I think back on the remarkable run I have had in politics over the last 21 years. I have risen to a level I never thought possible, and a key ingredient to my success has been *The Insider*, a monthly newsletter I began almost 15 years ago. The positive feedback from readers over the years, often from people who were total strangers to me, made me realize the power of personal journalism.

I gladly accepted the burden of writing, producing and delivering the newsletter because I knew it had the power to move people.

Writing *The Insider* has satisfied my desire to emulate one of my first heroes—I. F. Stone, who produced *I. F. Stone's Weekly*, a 4-page newsletter for 20 years beginning in the 1950s. I wrote my Masters Thesis on Stone, and I feel lucky to have been able to adapt his format and launch a successful newsletter of my own. The hours spent on the computer, writing and rewriting the text, printing the copies on my risograph, and then feeding them thru my folding machine at late hours in my basement have been perversely enjoyable.

In this volume, I have collected what I think are the best of the articles I have written over the last decade. I hope you enjoy them, whether you are seeing them for the first time, or remembering them from long ago. Reading them over is almost like reading a diary of my life since I entered the legislature.

I have been especially fortunate to have the services of the daughter I never had, and the best intern ever, Ashley Morris, who taught me how to self-publish, layout, efficiently edit and organize this book. I have written about her skills at length in this book, and I could not have finished this tome without her tireless and patient work. She also helped me edit Larry McDonnell's *Six*, a biography of my maternal grandfather, which we completed about 3 months ago. This is Ashley's last project for me and I expect great things from her as she completes law school and her

Masters degree in Human Resources. I have every confidence that she will conquer the business world in short order.

I myself look forward to new challenges in academia in the days ahead. *The Insider* may yet live on. I enjoy producing it too much to stop right now. So long as readers continue to find value in it, I will be happy creating it.

I HATE THOSE MEESES TO PIECES

Mouse Wars Revisited

The call came in on my hotline late one evening.

It was my 78-year old mother, Nancy. She was highly agitated. Obviously, this was not one of the periodic tests we conduct to ensure our dedicated phone lines were properly functioning. The tremor in her voice convinced me that *this was no drill.*

"Condition Red," Nancy stammered. "They have breached the outer wall. They are marauding and pillaging throughout the cabinets. My position may be overrun."

"Remain calm," I suggested. "Advise evacuation immediately."

"Negatory," mom replied. "Escape route sealed off. Varmint has occupied the garage."

"I copy you," I barked, my mind racing. Obviously, Nancy's sense of duty forbid relinquishing the Switalski ancestral home. If the Mouse was to triumph, her warrior code required going down with the ship.

My mom described the particulars. Without warning, the Mouse had renewed hostilities in her kitchen cabinets. The conflict encompassed two theatres of operation, including all three cabinet shelves and the garage. Highly motivated *Mouse Regulars* had appeared on the field of battle in impressive numbers. The world had not seen such a relentless onslaught since human waves of Chinese poured across the Yalu during the Korean War.

"I'll begin full assault with a strike force in 45 minutes," I promised. "Over and out."

I assessed the situation.

After my last victory, I thought I'd achieved *Peace in our Time.* Unfortunately, the varmint does not know the meaning of the word *quit.*

I've faced the beast in protracted conflict three times, and this was to be the second battle for the *Motherland.* My mother's kitchen rivals the Balkans as one of the world's hot spots. As astute readers will recall, I commanded allied forces defending the *Motherland* from Varmint Cong in 1983. That campaign ended in the complete capitulation of the

Mouse Nation. But even after 21 years, it was now clear that pacification just hadn't taken hold.

Consequently, I live like the *Yanamamo* of *Tierra del Fuego,* a primitive tribe subsisting in a perpetual state of warfare.

Peace? There is no peace. Within the resolution of each conflict are the seeds, or better yet, the crumbs, of the next Great War.

I arrived at eleven hundred hours and surveyed the situation. After applying camouflage to my face, I pulled on my *balaclava* and tightened the snaps of my down coat. Although a second pair of gloves were called for in the field manual, I needed my quickness and dexterity. I ordered mom to withdraw and seal off the kitchen.

"Mind those cracks under the door," I hollered. She unrolled the visqueen and sealed off the kitchen with duct tape. I felt dizzy from lack of oxygen and the 160 degree bodyheat within the down jacket.

Armed with only a truncheon fashioned from a rolled up newspaper, I cautiously opened the cabinet. Grounds of coffee spilled out everywhere. I examined the killing ground. Heaps of coffee and sugar were strewn around the lower two shelves.

The varmints had run amok.

One casualty remained on the battlefield, caught in the minefield of traps behind the powdered sugar. Blood stained the wall where the trap had detonated. There was one prisoner, caught in a coffin-like clear plastic Mouse Motel. The one-way door lets the hungry soldier in to enjoy a piece of cheese, but there's no exit strategy.

I began to unload the vast quantity of food, spices and cooking staples from the three shelves. I wanted the entire sector emptied of contents. There would be no hiding places for the varmint. I wanted to engage my superior armaments with a full field of fire. Paraphrasing the Roman historian Tacitus, I would create a desert and call it peace.

I was working quickly when I caught a furtive movement from the corner of my eye.

I froze.

Slowly I withdrew, stepping down from the chair. I turned to face the movement, while switching the bludgeon to my right hand.

What was that?

Something was alive in that bag of flour.

Did this varmint dare attempt an ambush during mopping up operations? Fearing an attempt to liberate the prisoner, I executed same. I isolated the movement to an open 2-pound bag of Betty Crocker's enriched flour. Were these varmints so arrogant as to continue feasting while I was engaging them in full combat attire?

Was it a nest of varmints? Had they covered themselves in flour, in order to impersonate laboratory mice? The association reminded me of the dangers of biological warfare. These creatures might be hosting bubonic plague.

I tightened the drawstrings on my hood.

Through reconnaissance, I discovered a mouse had been caught in a trap, survived, and had fallen into the bag of flour, from which he was now attempting to extricate himself. Brandishing my newspaper menacingly, I removed the entire bag, with mouse enclosed, and disposed of the lot. Much flour was thereby wasted, but such is the insane calculus of war.

I emptied the cabinets and set six traps.

I called my mother in and was explaining the battle plan when we heard a loud snap.

These beasts were bold indeed. After only a few minutes we'd caught the evening's fourth mouse. He stared at me with an unblinking evil eye, a pale brown eye with a film over it. *My blood ran cold.* Moved by equal combinations of pity and terror, I decided to let him die in darkness. I closed the door and concluded the briefing with my mother. Returning to dispose of the carcass, I found he had escaped. I cursed myself for not dispatching him on the spot. Now I would have to do battle with this miscreant again. And next time it might be on *his terms.*

I paused to reflect.

The policy of containment had failed. The Mouse had gone underground, building his organization for a generation, until he had reached sufficient strength. Now he had achieved breakout capability. Would the struggle ever end? Did my individual victories mean nothing? Was my life to be defined as one long fight against the varmint? Would my years of toil in Academe, rising to the heights of the Corporate World, and my record of distinguished service in the Public Sector ultimately mean nothing?

I peered into the future and read my epitaph.

Here lies Michael Switalski.
He Fought the Mouse and the Mouse Won.

I redoubled my efforts.

The bloody campaign had raged for a fortnight, with 14 mice Killed in Action when I was called in to interrogate a suspicious looking prisoner. I peered into his detention motel and activated the karaoke machine for questioning. The captive was greasy looking, with wet, black, oily hair and pointed ears, much unlike the furry brown rodents we'd been dealing with.

I smelled a rat.

He stood mute during the interrogation, for which provocation he paid the ultimate price. Meanwhile, our homeland security audit revealed the entry point for the terrorist mice. The tube feeding the gas fireplace went thru a hole in the bricks just wide enough to permit varmint infiltration.

I sealed the hole along with a similar crack in the cabinet wall. That night I thought I heard the jingle of bells.

Hark! It was the beating of his hideous heart.

I'd succeeded in walling in the evil-eyed varmint who'd escaped me earlier. Trapped in the wall, he would perish in due time.

Nancy and I celebrated our victory with a glass of Amontillado.

Requiescat in Pace, Varmint.

February 2004

Return of the Varmint

"Mickey!" my wife Roma shouted excitedly. *"There's something in the fireplace!"*

"Yes, Dear," I countered. *"Those are called logs. It's a gas fire. They're fake logs."*

"No, you idiot!" she screamed. *"It is alive!"*

"Well, <u>real</u> logs <u>were</u> once alive," I explained patiently, *"but as I said, those are fake logs."*

*"Mickey! There is **an animal** in the fireplace!"*

"Why didn't you say so?" I gasped.

As I advanced quickly on the fireplace, I heard the distinctive sounds of an alien being. It was an evil, growling, snarling sound, like the *Hound of the Baskervilles.* And I could just make out the sound of powerful molars grinding human bones.

I halted immediately.

"Oh my God! Oh my God!" I pleaded, raising my hands to the heavens and invoking the Deity. *"We are under varmint attack! Battle Stations everyone! Prepare to repel the Intruder!"*

I turned to review the forces at my disposal.

Wife Roma, *Second in Command*, standing at attention, with her hands on her hips and her head moving in a strange side-to-side fashion.

Son Liam, *Communications Specialist*, brandishing a PSP (Play Station Portable).

Myself, *Supreme Allied Commander*, *Special Agent* with a *License to Kill Varmint*.

We took our positions.

Peeking over from behind the couch with my field glasses, I coolly surveyed the situation. We were in a complete type of situation. The varmint had penetrated the *sanctum sanctorum*, the holiest of holy places: *The TV Room*. The Enemy stood at the Gates. Only the thin glass doors of the fireplace separated him from *The Remote*. And those glass doors were loose. The frame had separated from the brick. Roma had been after me for years, perhaps the better part of a decade, to repair or replace those doors.

I had other priorities.

If I'd had the foresight to install a remote starter for the fireplace, we'd be having *BBQ-ed Badger* for dinner. Instead, I thought I could see the 250-pound *Rabid Raccoon* hurling himself at the doors. He was using one of the ceramic logs as a battering ram, which he clutched tightly with his razor sharp claws. He could easily breach our perimeter, bite thru our phone lines, sever all communications with the outside world, and drop a significant trail of varmint deposits along the way.

"We must stabilize the front!" I ordered. I dispatched Liam to the basement to procure a bludgeon, and snatched the long handled floor mop from a nearby corner and handed it to Roma.

"Liam," I called. *"If he gets out, club him to death with extreme prejudice. Roma, you secure the fireplace doors by pressing this mop against them. Use all your weight."*

"What is this thing?" asked Roma.

It was her first experience of any kind with a mop.

"Damn those cutbacks in training funds! Just keep him in there," I barked.

I deftly snatched the large Poinsettia sitting in front of the doors as I guided Roma's mop joust into position. The fireplace was dark inside, but I thought I could make out the shape of a large, man-eating *Wolverine* straining against the doors, pushing with his hind legs against the fake logs.

"The doors are temporarily secure," I announced. *"Bring forward combat equipment."*

The beast punctuated these preparations with a bellicose war-cry from deep within the fireplace. The language was raspy and gutteral.

"I smell Al Qaeda *,"* I warned.

Now I raced to the basement, returning with a large section of pegboard, two cinder blocks and an industrial strength gas spotlight. Liam had a 5-foot long oversized gavel, given to my brother at his judicial installation, and a wooden rifle that shoots rubber bands. Thick rubber bands.

"We need proper intelligence on the enemy," I began. *"Roma, hold those doors tight. Liam, stand by with the gavel. And give me that rifle."*

Rubber bands in place, I gripped the spotlight with my free hand. Perhaps we could flush our quarry with a fury of light and sound.

"OK Liam," I ordered, *"Put on your Ludacris CD and turn it up to 11."*

I bathed the fireplace in high-intensity blue xenon light.

"I see him!" I exclaimed above the din. *"There's his tail on the floor. It's a mammoth possum!"*

Terror gripped our steadfast trio.

"He's hiding behind the logs," I warned. *"He's a big one. And they're strong. We push him, he may decide to take out the gas line and blow the whole house."*

I snifted the air cautiously.

"See his tail hanging below?" I continued. *"I saw it move."*

It was long, bald and sickly white in color, tapering at the end. It seemed smooth, but scaly, like a rat-tail. And though it hung limp, I could imagine the power of its grip. Easily enough to choke a man.

"That's a stick, Dad," said Liam calmly.

"There he goes now, he just went up the flue," said Roma. *"It's a squirrel."*

We regrouped.

I changed the Color-Coded Electronic Alert Board above the fireplace from **Red—Varmint Attack Underway** to **Orange— Varmint Prepared to Strike**, and told my troops to stand down.

"This isn't over, soldiers. We must enhance the security of our perimeter," *I ordered.* "While we entrench, the enemy may attempt a breakout. If the varmint escapes, we must confine him to the family room and kitchen. We cannot allow him access to our rear echelon."

I closed the sliding door to the living room, and we upended the kitchen table and sealed off the hallway leading upstairs. I opened the sliding glass door out to the back yard patio.

"We have to allow the varmint the opportunity to retreat with dignity," I explained.

Roma's arms were turning blue, either from the cold or from holding the mop.

On my signal, she withdrew the mop as Liam and I snapped the pegboard in place, securing it against the doors with the cinderblocks. This occurred in seconds, to the intensified verbal objections of the monster within.

But I worried about the small holes in the pegboard. Could the captured demon take the form of smoke, stream thru the holes in the pegboard, and reconstitute itself inside the room as a sharp-fanged wolf?

By now the temperature had plunged to minus-7 Celsius in the family room. Thinking we could make quick work of the invader, I hadn't bothered to change from my T-shirt and lounge pants.

I shivered.

Now I knew how the Germans felt at Stalingrad.

I closed the patio door.

A quick meeting of the War Council yielded a consensus on bringing in mercenaries for the final assault. We checked the yellow pages under "Soldier of Fortune," and after several calls, an accomplished assassin, Agent Neeley, appeared at our door. Armed with a steel cage and a stale jelly donut, a large black squirrel was our prisoner the next morning.

"If you just let him out, he'll come right back down the chimney," I predicted, secretly cursing Michigan's Constitution that bans Capital Punishment. "I think we should consider *extraordinary rendition.*"

"We'll be taking him in for open-ended interrogation," Agent Neeley said brusquely. He eyed the creature's fingernails menacingly.

"Suit yourself," I responded. "He deserves what he gets. And those animal rights people are soft on terrorism, anyway."

January 2006

Alien Mouse Resurrection
The Rebecca Agostino Chronicles

Be afraid.

Be very, very afraid.

I thought I was secure in *Fortress Switalski*, my Roseville estate made impregnable to the frequent onslaughts of mice, squirrel, and other alien varmint.

I was wrong.

I forgot about my allies. Alliances normally *increase* security. But a chain is only as strong as its weakest link. As usual, that link is my younger brother Matt.

He failed to acknowledge the warning signs. There were droppings, the nibbled corners of the Little Caesar's boxes in the garage. Most telling had been the firefight with mice at his *Pintail Grill* a year ago. Matt ignored these signs. He felt safe under the shade of my security umbrella.

Fool!

The Mouse is on the move again.

Seeking to disrupt the *Thanksgiving Holiday*, a way station for his *Plot to Destroy Christmas*, the Mouse began with a sneak attack on an isolated outpost along the frontier in Clinton Township. Amid the barren empty moorlands of *Partridge Creek Subdivision*, there sits a lonely pioneer settlement, surrounded by vast varmint breeding grounds.

The distress signal came late on T-Day minus 2, the Tuesday before Thanksgiving.

Matt needed a bailout.

He and his wife, Rebecca Agostino, were preparing their vehicle, a Ford Edge, for takeoff. Destination: My sister Jeannie's house in the Thumb, site of the *Switalski Family Thanksgiving Dinner*. Rebecca was in the Captain's chair.

Suddenly an *Intruder* leapt out of the dashboard vent straight at her jugular. Their eyes met for an instant, but all Rebecca could recall later, under hypnosis, were two beady eyes and yellow, razor sharp incisors. Interpol matched this description to an *Alien Mouse*, ignoring a 2nd positive ID for Matt.

With the Mouse in mid-air, Rebecca instinctively recoiled to the left. She took a glancing blow to the shoulder from the 2-inch *Alien*. Before the mouse could warp his long tail around her neck and leap down her throat, she executed a deft *ju jitsu* move and slammed him to the car floor.

The *Alien* scurried up and over Matt, who was curled up in a fetal position on the passenger seat, and disappeared in the aft section of the craft.

Reconstructing the crime scene, Lab technicians proved that a 2-inch mouse would need the hind legs of a kangaroo to leap the 2 feet to Rebecca's shoulder. Clinton Township Police were put on alert for this half-mouse, half-kangaroo or *kangarouse*. As such, we warned them the *alien hybrid* might also have been carrying a tiny, 2 centimeter baby *kangarouse* in its pouch.

Back at ground zero, Matt and Rebecca took quick action.

Armed with brooms and bludgeons, they emptied the car, but the *Alien* was nowhere to be found. Matt suspected he was hiding in the ductwork of the air handling system. He donned a nuclear suit, complete with visor, and drove the vehicle to a service station specializing in *Alien* extraction.

Matt's weapon of choice against varmints is Fire. When mice invaded his outdoor grill last Spring, he BBQ'd them on the spot. This time, Technicians assisted him in supercharging the heating system, achieving core temperatures of nearly 2000 degrees.

"I think we got him," Matt told me. "He couldn't take that heat. Either he evacuated, or we've got Mouse Jerky somewhere in the ducts."

Matt was confident, but without the corpse, there was no way to be sure the car was *Alien-Free*.

And given Rebecca's encounter with the *Alien*, some feared she might have become an unwitting "host" and that a *kangarouse* might burst forth from her stomach during the turkey and gravy portion of the evening.

This posed a dilemma. Many in the family have been secretly hoping for a 3rd child, a boy, to join Matt and Rebecca's lovely

daughters Gigi and Sophia. But we were unwilling to have this addition be a half-man, half-mouse *Alien* bent on the destruction of the earth.

We held an emergency session of the SSC, the *Switalski Security Council* up in Harbor Beach, where Jeannie was stuffing the turkey. No minutes were kept, but the SSC subsequently issued an unsigned order for a quarantine of Matt's family. Neither they nor the Ford Edge was to enter the 1000 yard perimeter surrounding Jeannie's Farmhouse unless the severed head of the mouse was sent ahead by courier. Alternatively, the entire dead mouse carcass could be secured to the roof of the vehicle, like a deer, to demonstrate *bona fides*.

This was cruel, but having commandeered the Ford Edge, who is to say the *kangarouse* might not penetrate the Saturn Vue, or the Doge Caravan? Once aboard, the concealed alien could hitch a ride to our home base, disembark under cover of night, and lay siege to our living quarters and destroy our economy.

We needn't have worried. Matt, Rebecca and the girls were too paralyzed by fear to reenter the car. They spent Thanksgiving isolated at home under Mouse Arrest.

Thus did Fear ruin our holiday.

Be afraid.

Be very, very afraid.

Of fear itself.

December 2008

Mouse Hunt III

My party was going to start in five minutes.

My brother Matt and I were putting the finishing touches on our rudimentary decorations. It was almost 8 o'clock. I walked into the bathroom to wash my hands. Matt turned white and froze.

"D-D-Did you see that?" he stammered.

"What?"

"M-M-mouse," he gasped, quivering.

"Where?"

"It ran out the door when you went in there."

"Where'd it go?"

"In the corner there, under the file cabinet."

"Give me the broom," I ordered. "I'm gonna terminate that mouse with extreme prejudice."

This was no idle boast. I have a sobering record of mousicides.

The mouse, knowing his end was near, bolted for the back bathroom and disappeared under the door. I flicked on the light and just caught a glimpse of him as he scurried thru a crack in the wall.

"I haven't seen a retreat that fast since the Taliban left Kabul," I told Matt. "He won't be back."

"How do you know that?" he cried. "You should stuff some paper in that crack."

I tried to reassure him. He's passed out before on lesser provocation.

"I'll leave the light on and crank the music up. See that?" I asked, gesturing toward the stereo. "This new amplifier goes up to eleven. That's beyond the mouse's aural pain threshold. Color him gone."

"How do you know that?" he blubbered again.

His panic was becoming tiresome.

"He can't handle the noise," I reasoned. "It worked with Noriega."

Matt wasn't buying it. "I just want the truth!" he demanded. "What if he comes back?"

Just then the bells jingled on the front door as our first guest arrived.

"If he comes back, he comes back. Keep this broom handy," I told him. "I have to greet our guests."

After midnight, the hunt was on. It was time to make war on the varmint.

My first objective was to assemble an alliance against the creature. Unilateralism never solves anything. It would serve no purpose if I rooted out the varmint's network in my office, only to see him set up safe havens in my neighbor's offices on the other side of the wall.

I sent a communication to the other tenants. Anyone caught harboring the varmint would be considered fellow vermin. You either join me in the coalition against the mouse or I move for your eviction.

Next I turned to the homefront. I feared Matt would waver if the fight got too tough.

"Matthew," I said. "You are the weakest link. Goodbye!"

In his stead, I enlisted the most bloodthirsty soldier available. I summoned my 8-year old son Liam from his Nintendo 64 controller, ending his slaughter of Donkey Kong critters at some 10,957 casualties.

My coalition assembled, I now turned my attention to the varmint. How engineer his demise?

I retired to the Situation Room and began my research. The Roseville Theatre was built in 1929. It's a historic building. I compared 1929 with the current date, December, 2001.

"Aha!" I exclaimed. "This tribe of mice has been here for two centuries! We're talking traditional society here," I explained to Lieutenant Liam. "We've got to return to the origin of the species. We've got to sweep away 100 years of pro-mouse

propaganda! We've been brainwashed by Disney with Mickey Mouse and Stuart Little. This mouse is the Evil One."

I pondered my alternatives while a wary Lieutenant Liam hid his Stuart Little video from me. This would be classic asymmetric warfare. Man against Mouse.

Deferring to the ancients, I retrieved several dusty tomes from my library. This being the Year of the Rat in China, I first read Lao Tzu's *The Art of War*. But Von Clausewitz' famous dictum seemed even more prescient. This war would literally be the continuation of politics by other means.

I consulted Machiavelli. My enemy's enemy is my friend. Hmmm. Should I bring in mercenaries? A cat might just do the trick. But then what? The victorious cat might feel entitled to take up permanent residence. Unthinkable. The feline proxy war died in its conceptual phase.

Next I ruled out Biowarfare. There'd be too many complications with my gutless allies.

How about Cyberwar?

At first blush, this seemed promising. 21st century man versus traditional mouse. I liked my odds. Then again, I might be pitting myself against the mouse's strength. Although seemingly primitive, mice have actually gone hi-tech. Reliable statistics suggest at least 99% of computers are equipped with a mouse. That's a formidable network.

I finally settled on a staple of conventional warfare, a variant on the landmine. Committed to the low-tech option, I unearthed two mousetraps from my basement storage, surplus from my last encounter with the varmint.

I laid my traps, baiting them with yogurt, a traditional food from the East.

Nothing doing. The traditional society mouse had apparently given way to a thoroughly modern mouse. This mouse had apparently been corrupted by the fast food of the infidels.

I changed tactics.

Undisclosed intelligence sources revealed to Liam the true identity of my foe. The Evil One was none other than the Frito Bandito. I got some Fritos, smeared them with peanut butter, and reset the traps.

Success was immediate.

The mouse has been vanquished, and as promised, the troops were home before Christmas.

Buoyed by another victory, I confidently erected my Office Xmas tree. Finally, I could enjoy the Holiday Season in comfort and satisfaction.

It was the night before Christmas, and all through the house, not a creature was stirring.

Not even a mouse.

January 2002

FAMILY MATTERS

The Mother of All Battles

I had been brooding for months.

My mother, Nancy, had left Roseville, my lifelong home.

She had been spirited away by my baby brother Matthew, and was living in *Babylonian Captivity* in Clinton Township behind the Partridge Creek Mall.

She sold the Switalski ancestral home on Martin Road, built by my late father, Norbert, some 45 years ago.

I couldn't argue with the logic of the move. In fact, I supported it. Nancy was 83. The house was a two-story, four-bedroom colonial. She lived there alone, and her bedroom was on the second floor while the laundry was in the basement. Nancy's knees were shot from years of hand-delivering my political literature. Her kids, myself included, had all grown up and moved out. So it made perfect sense when one day she casually mentioned that she was contemplating downsizing.

Matt swooped in. He and his wife Rebecca were building a new house in tony Partridge Creek. They finished off the basement into a luxurious lower flat, complete with private entrance, a full kitchen, and bath. It even had windows. They quickly enticed my mother into their home, with the added bonus of being with her two grandchildren, Gianna, 3, and Sophia, 1.

My devious brother had executed a deft *fait accompli*. Nancy had left the 'ville and was ensconced in splendor in the nether regions of a Northern Clinton Township McMansion.

I accepted Matt's sophisticated kidnapping with outward indifference.

Inwardly, it didn't sit right with me. I kept my own counsel and secretly plotted my mother's return. After all, Nancy had lived in Roseville for over 50 years. My universe would be out of sync until she returned.

I unleashed my master plan patiently, unobtrusively, to allay any possible suspicions. I would invite my mother to late night parties at my house, ply her with bourbon and cokes, and then insist that she not drive home. After all, I had a comfortable four-bedroom colonial myself, in Roseville, and with only me, my wife Roma, and son Liam, we had two spare bedrooms.

I invited her to spend holiday weekends at the house, and she occasionally accepted.

After months of laying the groundwork, I told her I enjoyed having her around. I casually suggested that she move in.

Nancy, playing hard to get, was non-committal. But I may have overplayed my hand. The word was out, and Matt became aware of my designs.

The competition began a new phase.

The race was on to sign the *Greatest Free Agent* in history.

Forget about A-Rod. Forget about C.C. Sabathia.

This free agent was Nancy Ann McDonnell, out of Salina, Kansas, graduate of Marymount College, Majorette, mother of 7, former Roseville Councilwoman, the "Super-Sub" teacher at Roseville High School, pianist, bon vivant and matriarch of the Switalski Clan. Still gainfully employed at *Nickel and Saph Insurance* and scourge of her monthly Bridge Club.

Attempts to reach an accommodation with her current "team" were inconclusive. I refused to pay Matt's insistent demands for severance fees.

"She's a free agent," I bellowed. "I am not buying out her contract from you. She can sign with anyone she pleases."

Tensions mounted. Ever resourceful, Matt started coaching his two beautiful daughters, Gianna and Sophia. "Tell Grandma you want her to stay here forever," he cooed, using unscrupulous guilt-trip tactics.

My position was eroding.

Matt's insidious tactics were working. I had to put together a lucrative package, even if I had to give away the store. As my friend Bruno Fuciarelli once told me: "You can have many *wives*, but there is only one *mama*."

Luckily, I wouldn't be losing my wife over this one. Roma was in full support of the acquisition. She loves my ma, but at times I suspected that her motives were not entirely pure.

In fact, she smelled blood.

As we put together our incentive package, my wife kept inserting home makeover projects that I had successfully delayed or vetoed for years. "We need new carpeting on the steps," she observed. "Otherwise your mother might slip."

I nodded.

"We should get new windows," she warned. "It might be drafty for Nancy."

To keep a united front, I now had to accede to Roma's demands. She saw our bid for Nancy as an opportunity to get the *new kitchen* she had lusted after for years.

Awakened by a nightmare, I sat up in bed, alone in the darkness, drenched in sweat. Do you have *any idea* what a *new kitchen* costs?

I had no choice but to agree.

There was something in this for everybody. Even my son, Liam, wrangled a TV in his bedroom, since he would no longer be able to monopolize the family room TV, programmed to some obscure European soccer games, for 18 hours a day.

At this rate, soon it would be *me* relegated to the basement. I schemed to offer my *Spectacular Bid* without further delay.

One night, after Sunday Family Dinner, I ordered the women and children upstairs and Matt, Nancy and I sat down at mom's kitchen table for some hard bargaining on *final status* negotiations. I had to move quickly and decisively, lest my four thieving sisters get wind of these machinations and attempt to lure my mother to one of *their homes* out of state. Clinton Township was one thing. Maryland, Rhode Island or Florida was completely unacceptable.

I began confidently, laying out a lucrative package of benefits.

"First of all, mom, I think you should be in Roseville. You've lived your whole life there. All your friends are there. You still go to church there. People there are always asking me about you. They miss you."

From under the table, I cued the soft violins with the CD remote.

"But here's what I have to offer," I continued, picking up the pace. "When you walk in my front door, immediately to your right is the living room and attached dining room. They are spacious, with newly finished wood floors and the bulk of my *Gonzo* art collection. All this is yours, to do whatever you want with. That's your apartment. You have a door to the kitchen, and I have procured the antique French Doors from *Phil's Pharmacy* in Mount Clemens, courtesy of my friend, Pat Chownyk. I will install them according to your specifications at the entrance from the front hall. That is your space and you can have privacy there whenever you want it."

"But there is more," I added. "Upstairs, you get the *Yellow Bedroom*, which is the largest bedroom in the house, complete with walk-in closet."

"That is in addition," I reminded her triumphantly, "to your suite of rooms downstairs, to which we will install your own cable outlet."

I glanced at Matt. He was turning white.

"Did I mention," I added brusquely, "that you get a parking spot in the garage, and it's the one closest to the door?" Left unsaid was the fact that Matt had mom parking on the street, like a common lodger.

You need allies in putting together an attractive package, and we'd left no stone unturned. "Our next-door neighbors, Shelly and Joe Boedeker, are due to have their baby this summer,' I continued. "Shelly will bring the wee boy around for a walk in our high pram. And she says she will serve you wine whenever you want in their hot tub."

"Bourbon and Coke!" Nancy blurted out.

It was the signal I needed. I now moved in for the *coup de grace*.

"Finally, I offer this all to you **rent-free.**"

My spies had discovered that Matt was secretly charging my mother rent.

"That's just utility money," protested Matt defensively.

"Whatever," I shrugged. "You don't have to pay utilities with me, either."

The jig was up.

Matt threw his hands up into the air, a pained look of betrayal on his face. "I can't compete with that," he cried.

I could tell I'd won. The only thing left was to assure mom she wouldn't be hurting Matt and Rebecca's feelings by signing with me. Plus it was time for me to salvage a few scraps from the negotiations.

"I require only that you make dinner once a week," I observed, "and Sunday Dinner doesn't count." Even after being showered with goodies, everyone likes to know their talents are appreciated.

"And I must admit I have my own purposes in wanting you to live with me," I confided. "I have made my decision about what I am going to do when my term expires at the end of 2010. I am going to run for Congress. I need you mom, to help me. You can do my correspondence. You love doing that and you are good at it. Will you take this one last journey with me? I really need you."

"See!" Matt rallied, accusingly. "He's going to make you work 65 hours a week without pay!"

"Not a minute more than 56 hours," I countered. "Seriously, Mom, I need you. Will you help me!"

She had to say yes.

Nothing compares to being needed. Not even a parking spot next to the door.

But it was more than that.

Simply put, I love my mother, and she loves me.

Nancy moves in with us this month.

It's like the Fat Man told Sam Spade. "If you lose a son, you can get another. But there is only one *Maltese Falcon*."

July 2009

Divine Secrets of the YaYa Brotherhood

My little brother Matt, *aka* Judge Matthew Switalski, recently married at the tender age of 34. I though he'd never leave my mother's house. He had it pretty good there as the baby of 7 kids. But the combination of rent and the love of the beautiful Rebecca Agostino proved irresistible for Matt.

Matt honored me by asking me to be his best man at his May wedding. Part of my traditional duties included the staging of a *Stag Nite*.

But Matt is unique. Instead of the traditional rite of passage involving an evening of *heavy drinking, gambling and womanizing,* Matt envisioned something different.

His initial plan of jetting to Britain to see a couple of soccer games proved unfeasible. The fallback involved Matt and I driving to Washington DC for a long weekend to see Congress, the Supreme Court, the Monuments, Arlington, and Gettysburg. Matt is a man of ideas, and our pilgrimage to these shrines promised to fire his imagination more than the DVD version of *Spring Break.*

The trip got off to a rocky start when the 7-hour, 500 mile drive turned into a 14-hour, 800 mile wander through the wilderness. We don't like to talk about it, because what went on during those lost hours should properly remain a mystery. Let's just say you normally go from Michigan to Ohio to Pennsylvania to Maryland. We will stipulate that documentary evidence exists showing our vehicle traversed State of New York toll roads. We offer no comment on the infamous 14-hour gap.

We take our inspiration from Henry Ford II. In the words of Hank the Deuce, *"Never complain, never explain."*

We can talk about DC. Congress was out of session, so we could not enter the actual House and Senate chambers. But the Cherry Blossoms around the tidal basin were in full bloom, truly a sight to behold. We got into the Supreme Court Chambers, but missed the historic Affirmative Action case by two days. We went to Camden Yards to see the Orioles get pounded 12-2 while we pounded down Boogus Burgers with my sister Moe and her family.

Carolyn Hadgikosti, who is not only the granddaughter of *Lindell AC* owner Johnny Butsicaris, but also my next door neighbor, and beyond that a valued member of Congressman Sandy Levin's Washington staff, escorted us on a great tour of the Capitol and the Court.

When she offered to take us out for a tour of the monuments that evening, we jumped at it. We arranged to meet for dinner and the monuments at the *Old Ebbits Grill*, where General Ulysses S. Grant used to drink.

Matt and I proceeded to Arlington. It's build on a farm confiscated from Robert E. Lee, and includes Lee's house, which sits high atop a hill with a great vista of downtown Washington. Nearby are the graves of President Kennedy and Jackie, with the eternal flame. A stone's throw away is the grave of Robert Kennedy, provocative in its simplicity. A small white cross and plain headstone mark his grave, and across the way his eloquent words call us to fight for justice. The cemetery closed at 5, so we caught the metro to *Old Ebbits*.

We were an hour early.

We'd been up all night, a table was available, and we were starving.

So we ate.

This was a problem. We'd promised Carolyn and her friend dinner. Now we'd gorged ourselves without them.

What to do?

Pretend we hadn't eaten. We quickly paid our bill and snuck up to the front of the restaurant to meet Carolyn and Jennie. By now *Ebbits* was packed.

We met Carolyn and she got in line for a table. Matt and I hid back in the crowd, so the hostess wouldn't recognize us. She told Carolyn it would be an hour before we got a table.

"Let's go do the monuments first," I insisted. "When we come back they won't be as crowded."

Carolyn and Jamie weren't too keen on the idea, plus they were dressed to the nines. But I was determined. Matt pulled me aside.

"These poor girls have been working all day. They want to eat," he confided, weakly.

"I can't eat another dinner right now," I told him. "I've got to walk that salmon off. You give me an hour and a half of walking and I'll crush that menu."

The ladies finally agreed to take us on the tour, and so began the *Affair of the Two Dinners.*

We enjoyed the Jefferson, Lincoln, Korean, and Vietnam Memorials. The chiseled words of Lincoln at Gettysburg and the Second Inaugural are always inspiring. And walking thru the Vietnam Memorial is like experiencing the War all over again.

I could do without the new FDR memorial, a sprawling monstrosity of pavement and stone blocks that covers what seems like two-thirds of the tidal basin. After walking thru 3 or 4 huge plazas, I thought that was it. "No," explained Carolyn. "That was just one term. We have 3 more to go!"

We returned to *Old Ebbits Grill,* and a table was ready. Matt and I worried we'd get the same waiter, but luckily we were seated in an entirely different section of the restaurant.

Our ruse was succeeding. I became giddy.

During orders, I added an appetizer to demonstrate how famished I was. I questioned the waiter about the sweet potato soup, which I had just eaten two hours earlier. "My, that sounds magnificent," I gushed. "I'll try that!"

Emboldened I began gesticulating wildly with my spoon. "This is delightful," I announced, to no one in particular. "I must try this again, sometime." Matt was struggling, but with a Herculean effort I managed to clean my plate. We dodged the waitstaff on our way out, and skulked past the hostess to freedom.

Carolyn and Jennie were delightful company. "We'll take you somewhere else next time we come," I told them. "The portions there are *so meager.*" I began to insist that we return to the restaurant, in order that I might lodge a formal complaint with the hostess, but the hour was late and the ladies had to working in the morning. They begged me to suffer the wrong. I reluctantly acquiesced.

Matt and I proceeded to the train station. We'd missed the last train by 5 minutes.

We took a cab to Baltimore Park and Ride, and got lost again driving home.

Our trip ended with a full day at Gettysburg, visiting the battle sites and enjoying a custom tour from a New England banker who has made study of the war his hobby. All the way back to Michigan, all 7.5 hours, we listened to the Teaching Company's taped lectures on the History of the Civil War.

It was a great trip.

I'll always remember it fondly.

Especially the 18-hour gap.

June 2003

Unto Us A Child Is Born

On Tuesday, January 3rd a new Switalski was welcomed into the world.

By younger brother Matthew and his wife, Rebecca Agostino, are the proud parents of a baby girl, Gianna, who weighed in at 8 pounds and 4 ounces, and was 21 inches long. Mother and Baby are doing fine, and after a few anxious moments, we think Matt is going to survive also.

Matt doesn't have the strongest of stomachs. The sight of blood can send him swooning. He appeared a bit grey around the gills on B-Day, but Rebecca reports that he was a great help in the birthing room at St. Joe's Mercy in Clinton Township.

Rebecca and Matt are old fashioned. Even though they had an ultrasound and the technicians could see if it was a boy or a girl, they didn't want to know. Gianna's gender was a mystery until she was born. "I can't imagine doing it any other way," Matt told me. "It just brings home to you what a miracle the whole experience of birth is." Modern Science and Medicine have made great advances, and have the power to unlock great mysteries. But this final surprise reminds us of the miracle of creation.

Gianna is very beautiful, good natured, and has dark curly hair. Her grandmother Marcy is already planning to pierce her ears, a Mexican tradition. Gianna is also independent of spirit. I told Matt to be sure to have the baby before January 1st, and that way you would get a full year's tax deduction for the new dependent. But Gianna wanted to be born on her own timetable.

So figure $3200 on both state and federal forms, plus $600 bonus from the state, and that's $7000 in deductions a year for 18 years, plus a few extra years while she is in college, and that's $150,000 plus interest. Not quite a million dollar baby, but a serious chunk of change. But on second thought, I am sure Matt and Rebecca would have paid twice that, because the extra time in the oven often leads to a healthier baby.

Besides, you have to be impressed with Gianna's public spirit. While the rest of us are figuring ways to chisel the government out of a few extra dollars, Gianna did the responsible thing and paid her fair share of taxes. She is a good example to all of us.

Aren't good schools, good health care and public safety worth paying for? Or do tax cuts and tax avoidance trump those every time?

Not in Gianna's world, and not in mine, either.

January 2006

Will Ye No Come Back, Jenny?

My 87-year old Scottish mother-in-law, Janet McPhie Heaney, is nearing the end of her three-month visit to my home in Roseville. My wife Roma, my son Liam, and I especially will be sad to see Jenny go.

I would love for her to stay with us longer, but visits longer than 90 days now require a Visa from the US Customs and Immigration Service. To avoid the hassles, we decided a three-month visit would be adequate.

Jenny is from the auld school. She gets up early every day, and cleans the house all day, until she goes to bed about 9:30 pm.

Jenny is an outstanding organizer. She tackled the junk drawer, and rearranged the linen closet, folding all the towels and perfectly stacking them by size and color. She is 87, but she brought order to the chaos of cleaning supplies, sponges and rags under the kitchen sink, not the most comfortable area to work in. She then duplicated that feat with every other sink in the house, including under the basement set tubs.

I returned from Lansing one day to find her cleaning out the garage, and she tripled the area of usable space in our basement. And that was all the first week.

The pantry now features perfectly arranged cans, spices, and daily supplies, and we now easily find what we are looking for. Jenny would never throw anything away without our approval, so we ok'd the disposal of the 20-year old can of spam and the stale dated 6-pack of Billy Beer. Jenny has given every room in the house a thorough cleaning.

Even the Lord rested on the Seventh Day. But Jenny never rests. She collects all the dirty clothes each day, launders and folds them and places them, carefully sorted and arranged, on our beds. That includes matching the socks. She makes all the beds, and scolds me if I make Roma's and mine, because, as she often said, *"Michael, you have much more important things to be doing. Leave these wee footery things to me."* I am likewise discouraged from loading or unloading the dishwasher, or clearing the table, or doing any one of a hundred household chores. As you can imagine, I have protested mightily against these restrictions, to no avail.

I have since chosen to calmly accept my fate.

Jenny works harder than any person I have ever known. She raised five children in Scotland, and has been a fantastic grandmother to her 12 grandchildren and 5 great grandchildren. She has gone to all of Liam's soccer games and basketball games, although she protests after each game that she can't go again because it is just *"too exciting."* She loves sports, and went with us to a Pistons game during the preseason. She enjoyed it more than I thought she would, and marveled at the skills of the players.

Family means everything to Jenny. Her idea of a great evening, when she can be dissuaded from cleaning, is to watch interminable videotapes of Liam as a baby. She likes movies, too, and prefers Hollywood classics from the 40's and 50's, and is a big fan of John Wayne's *The Quiet Man.*

She loved dancing in her day. She married Harry Heaney, her late husband, in Glasgow where they lived for 55 years. Harry joined the Labour Party at the tender age of 17, when he should have been goofing around. He spent a life in politics in Scotland, and was a great guy. I have told his story in these pages before. Jenny's one disappointment in Harry was that he never learned to dance.

Jenny is also a huge music fan, and one of the highlights of her trip was going to the *Detroit Opera House* to see one of her favorites, *La Boheme*, with me, Roma, my mother Nancy and Jenny's other daughter Helena. Jenny cried when poor *Mimi* met her fate, and rose to reward the performers with vigorous applause. Sometimes I put opera on for her when she is working around the house. But she also enjoys modern music, and has long been far more knowledgeable about *British Pop* than her daughter Roma.

As her son-in-law, I can do no wrong. Whenever I return from a difficult afternoon of golfing, she insists that I lie down on the couch and urges my wife to get me something to drink because "Poor Michael must be exhausted." She takes my side in every dispute, and often tells Roma that she doesn't appreciate how good she has it.

I have tried telling Roma that for 21 years.

Cooking is about the only thing Jenny doesn't like to do. This is only because she doesn't think she is a great cook. She will eat anything you give her without complaint, and enjoys many cups of hot tea during the day. After 80-odd years of drinking tea with milk, she had some, for the first time, with lemon and honey, and thought it was fantastic.

Jenny is not hard to please.

As you can imagine, she is much sought after. My six brothers and sisters have all made application for her to stay with them, requests that I have curtly vetoed. We are very happy to keep her to ourselves, thank you. We know we don't deserve her, but we have managed to reconcile ourselves to that.

Roma will take Jenny back to Scotland soon, and entropy will begin to dissemble her monumental achievements in our home.

I am already beginning work on that travel Visa.

December 2005

Renovating the Pyramids

When the economy is slow, we all tend to hold off on discretionary spending. If you are already cheap like me, that just reinforces a natural tendency. I have been delaying, stalling, and otherwise dragging my feet on home improvement projects for years, much to my wife Roma's dismay.

So the omens were inauspicious for Roma's list of major projects. But my red-headed wife, like her mother Jenny, is tireless and determined.

I finally assented to having our ancient linoleum and threadbare carpet replaced with wood floors. The work went quickly, and the floors looked beautiful.

Too beautiful.

"Honey," cooed my wife. "Look how dingy that baseboard looks. We should paint that before they put the shoe molding on." I was struck with terror as visions of paint costs and painter fees ballooned before my eyes.

"Uh, yeah. Right," I stammered. As she reached for the phone to hire a painter, I blurted out "I'll run to the hardware store right now and get some paint. I'll get those baseboards done this weekend."

At 4 am Sunday morning, I crawled into bed, my body aching.

"Did you finish?" Roma yawned.

"Just a little touch up left," I assured her.

She put down the phone. Sunday evening, as I put away the last of the brushes and sandpaper, she called me over to the dining room.

"Look how bad those walls look," she observed, running the finger of her white gloved hand across the wall.

"I can get those," I promised. "It's gonna take a couple of weeks to finish."

"That's ok," Roma allowed. "I never noticed how many marks there are on that ceiling."

I pivoted.

"Well, while we have all the furniture in the garage, I could get the ceiling done," I suggested. "That might take a little time, but we can take our time and then get on the walls."

Roma eyed the phone menacingly.

"I can easily finish the ceilings this weekend, and get all the furniture back in," I promised. "I'll go get some ceiling paint now. I think there's a sale."

"While you're out, get one of those superflush toilets," Roma ordered. "I had them take out the toilet when they put in the bathroom floor."

The whole world started spinning around me. I felt faint. Roma took my hand reassuringly. "It's alright dear. I'll come with you."

The toilet went in with remarkable ease.

Too remarkable.

"Go back and get another one," commanded she who must be obeyed.

"Honey, this is a half bath. I don't think we can fit two in here," I reasoned. "Furthermore, although I love you, this is an activity I prefer to do in private."

"Not here you idiot," she rejoined. "The second one is for upstairs."

Done.

And while the floor replacement has mushroomed into a construction project rivaling the Great Pyramid at Giza, I feel that I am in my own small way helping to jump start the economy.

Besides, I got an email from Gaynell, my old girlfriend in Louisiana, who is a widow and is tearing out the sheetrock in her house by hand and chain sawing a fallen pecan tree in her backyard as a result of the devastations of Hurricane Katrina. She bathes in a stud walled shower with Christmas wrapping for a curtain.

Please ignore all my previous whining complaints about home improvement projects.

October 2005

The Importance of Family

By: Liam Switalski

Sixth-grader at St. Angela School in Roseville

I am an only child. I have no brothers or sisters. I have a mother and a father in my immediate family but I belong to a much bigger extended family. They make me feel like I am part of something very big and important.

I have 25 first cousins, 10 aunts, and 9 uncles. I have two grandmothers still alive. These 48 people are the family whom I spend vacations and holidays with. I have family all over the world: In Maryland, Rhode Island, Florida, Michigan, Canada and even in Scotland. My family comes to visit and stay with us often in Roseville. My family loves me for who I am and makes me feel special. They tell me stories that tell me where I came from and what my family means.

My Mum and Dad and I do something very special with my Dad's family every year. In the summer, we go on a vacation and sometimes some cousins from my mother's side of the family come with us. Most years 22 or more of us rent a large house for a week together. We have gone to the Carolinas, Maryland, Vermont, and Lake Michigan. Wherever we go we always have fun just being together as a family. We all take turns making our own kind of dinner for the whole group. I play all day with my cousins. My uncles and my dad organize a big soccer game and we play no matter the weather! My family teaches me competitiveness and fair play!

Most people have cousins that they know from birth. I also had the chance to get to know cousins who were adopted from Poland at ages 4, 5, and 6. These cousins, Sebastian, Basia and Jeanetta seem like my brother and sisters because we have become so close.

All of my family in Michigan tries to get together every Sunday for family dinner. We take turns hosting the dinner. We talk and my cousins and I play. We celebrate our birthdays and our accomplishments. My family makes me feel proud.

Although I do not get to see my Scottish family every week, I do spend every other Christmas and every other summer with them. Many of them come stay with us regularly. They have taught me about soccer (football to them) and that we do not all sound the same or do everything the same. They have lots of public transportation and I am able to go all over the city by bus and train with my cousins without my parents driving. I like the fact that I am Scottish as well as American.

I love my family very much. Despite the distances between us we still stay very close because we make the effort to get together as much as we can. My family has taught me values in life such as sportsmanship, sharing, caring for each other, and keeping together as a family. I am lucky to be Liam Heaney Switalski.

March 2005

Mick and the Beanstalk
It's a Jungle Out There!

True! Very dreadfully nervous, I have been, and am.

But why do you say that I am mad?

See how calmly I explain the whole thing to you. Are these the words of a madman?

I confess—readily—to an unnatural love of plants. Trees to be precise.

I have planted many perhaps too many—at my Garden of Eden in Shadowoods. After I filled every available hectare of soil with seedlings, my wife Roma expelled me from the Garden.

I was under strict orders. No more trees.

One Saturday I rose early and slipped away to Armada to the Macomb County Soil and Conservation District tree sale. I was gazing longingly at a hardwood packet and some fast-growing shade trees.

Then it happened.

A bearded, 4-foot man in a leather jerkin caught my eye. He looked like the Vernors gnome. He called to me with a mischievous grin.

"Three for a buck," he crowed. "It be a bargain what canny be beat."

"Three what?" I asked.

"Surely they be magic beans, my son," the gnome replied.

"They look like hybrid poplars to me," I sniffed, haughty in my horticultural wizardry.

"An even better bargain," cried the imp with delight. "You'll be made in the shade."

"Gimme dem beans," I ordered, thrusting a golden Sacagawea dollar into his tiny palm. "I've got the perfect spot for 'em."

Furtively, I smuggled the beans home.

"Hi, Honey," I greeted Roma upon my return. "I was just out delivering *The Insider*," I lied.

"You work so hard, dear," cooed Roma. "Sit down and let me make you some lunch."

That night, about midnight, while ostensibly taking out the garbage, I snuck to the side of the house and spilled the beans under a planting moon.

The deed was done.

My plan all along was to transplant the trees once they reached sufficient height to repel rabbits and hold their own against lawnmowers. Why else do you think I would plant them only 3 feet from the house? Do you think that I am mad?

Imagine my surprise when, within 3 years, they were already over my head. That fall I decided to take action, and got the shovel out. I set it next to the house, and the following Spring I began to dig.

Exhausted after two shovelfuls, I deferred action until the following fall.

They were now nearly 10 feet tall.

I tried furiously to dig them out.

Nothing doing.

The three trees were uncomfortably close to the house.

"They'll be fine," I explained to Roma. "They're a perfect fire escape for Liam if the house ever catches on fire. And they'll provide good shade for our southern exposure. It'll keep the house cool. Just think of how much we'll save on the air conditioning bill."

Roma considered my arguments, and ordered the trees removed.

I promised to get right on it.

Seven years later, the trees were well over 60 feet high.

The shade cover was so thick it was perpetually dark below, like a nuclear winter.

My Garden of Eden was barren.

Grass wouldn't even grow.

My Irish mother, Nancy Anne McDonnell, has a green thumb. She gave me a sprig of ivy she'd smuggled over from the Emerald Isle. She promised it was shade tolerant.

I planted it under the trees.

Before you can say Invasive Species it covered the ground and scaled the trees. The combination produced a major greenhouse effect. I was issued a provisional permit by the DEQ for CO2 emissions. I am a separate signatory to the Kyoto Treaty.

The burgeoning green canopy was so extensive that it was attracting its own weather patterns. Walking alongside my house was like entering a tropical rainforest. One day my longsuffering neighbor, Vi Hadjikosti, became ensnarled in the ivy, raspberry bushes, vines, dense undergrowth and poison nightshade. I heard her plaintive cries, and rescued her after hacking a swath towards her with my trusty machete.

Within an hour I got her loose. It was there that we made a blood pact against the greenery.

Vi launched an immediate blitzkrieg. With the help of her friend Mary, she leveled 4 large bushes obscuring her garage within a day. Then she thinned out the branches overhanging her yard.

Fiat Lux.

It was the First Day. And we saw that it was Good.

Now it was my turn.

I commandeered an upstairs bedroom for a command post.

I put black plastic over the windows to keep the trees from spying on my war plans. Veteran readers of *The Insider* will recall my successful campaigns against a variety of mammalian varmints.

But tiny mice, vicious and lethal though they be, are one thing.

I was up against three 70 foot monsters, larger than the greatest dinosaurs that ever roamed this planet. And these three Maneating Poplars, named Leviathan, Tyrannopoplar Rex, and Andre the Arbor, were far more dangerous than mere dinosaurs.

What they lacked in mobility, they made up for in bulk.

Roma and Vi urged me to call in Bounty Hunters.

Not a chance.

It would be wrong to pay someone to correct a problem I personally had created. I had planted the magic beans, and I alone would bring them to heel. I would perfect my control over my dominions, and I would not spend one penny in doing so. In the words of President Jefferson, scourge of the Barbary Pirates, *"Millions for Defense, but not one cent for Tribute."*

These trees were Toast. Er…firewood.

The Poplars were over 80 feet high, and there was only 20 feet of space between my house and Vi's. If I were to slay these dragons at one stroke, the falling carcass could level both of our houses. I hit upon a strategy of sectionalism. I would take the behemoths down, 5 feet at a time, until they were level with terra firma.

I climbed out my second story window with my son and squire, Liam. He held the ladder taking me to the 2nd floor roof. I was armed with a 15-foot extension pruner, with a little saw on the end.

I planned the attack carefully.

I had to wait until wind conditions were just right. Otherwise, the wind could blow the falling branches onto Vi's roof, and she might slap me with an injunction faster than you can say, *"Fee Fi Fo Fum."*

I straddled the roof and waved the pruner menacingly at the Poplars. They had me outnumbered. According to the ancient Chinese proverb, *The ax falls first on the tallest tree.* So I went after the biggest one, Leviathan, first. If I could defeat him, it would give me a psychological edge over the other two.

First I denuded Leviathan of all his branches with the pruner. Nakedness is demoralizing and made him more compliant with my wishes. I felt a tinge of vertigo as I straddled the crest of the roof and pruned off as many branches as I could reach. I wanted the top section to be as light as possible for the 40-foot fall to the ground.

I prevailed.

Next afternoon, my death match with Tyrannopoplar Rex drew a crowd, watching from the safety of the street. Straining on my tiptoes, I stretched to decapitate the top section at the highest possible point. Even so, the top section would still be 15 feet long.

To maximize the height of the cut, and steepen the angle, I stepped perilously close to the edge of the roof.

"Honey!" my wife screamed. "Be careful. Don't step on the roof vent or you might bend it."

I sawed with the Grim Reaper's saw for an hour and a half. My arms became so exhausted I could only take 10 strokes at a time before having to rest for a minute. After 3 days and many hours of sawing I had decapitated all three trees.

"Welcome to my world," I taunted the treetops as I dismembered them below. And not a moment too soon. I had achieved containment. Another 3 months and the Poplars would have grown beyond my reach.

I rotated out of the crucible of war for some R&R to recover from my exertions. Because of the way I had to cut, with my right arm and side doing all the work, my one half looked like Arnold Schwarzenegger, while my left side resembled Mini-Me.

After a week of relative relaxation logging at Sequoia National Park, I returned to the fray. I cut the behemoth trees down to 25 feet while standing on the roof, taking the rest of the summer to finish this stage of the campaign. As Fall began, I took them down to 18 feet, perched on an extension ladder with a hand saw. But the wood was so thick, and the blade so dull, that the work was becoming too exhausting.

For safety reasons, I didn't want to cut with a chainsaw while on the extension ladder, so I cut by hand down to 18 feet. Then I rigged a table with a ladder on top of it, solid enough to use the chain saw safely.

After I had cut through most of the tree, I descended and set the chain saw safely aside. I hand sawed the last inch until the tree was ready to topple. One last push would be enough. I had done this many times without incident.

I stood on the ladder and pushed the 5-foot section over. But it began to fall on a steeper angle than I had planned. Instead of falling directly away from me, it fell to my side. I watched its new trajectory as a casual observer might watch a distant bolt of lightning. But it was clear that it would hit the table upon which my ladder was erected.

The section swung down like a 2-ton pendulum, and struck the table with great force. It imparted a quarter moon gouge into the side of the table with a sickening crunch. It also sent the table flying 3 feet toward the house.

The ladder went with table. I however, standing on the ladder, was treated differently.

I did not fly to the right, like the table and ladder.

Although my feet did.

The rest of my body tipped to the left. I tried to grab the tree as I dropped, but I slid down the face of it, leaving a fair amount of the skin from my left arm on the bark. I hit the table just below my waist, and flipped heels over head onto the ground in a surprisingly soft landing. I came to rest at the bottom of the tree. My arm was scraped, and I had a few bruises, mostly to my ego. My chief concern was whether anyone had witnessed my acrobatics. I peered across the street to see if anyone noticed. The coast was clear. No sign of a video camera.

My secret was safe. I would not end up an unwilling buffoon on America's Funniest Home Videos.

The job completed, Roma and Vi greeted me as a conquering hero. My son Liam was impressed by my feat. I reduced the logs to kindling and stacked them at my brother Mark's house for firewood. So ended the saga of the trees.

How do you spell stumpgrinder?

November 2004

Nancy Switalski: Tough to Kill

Dedicated readers of *The Insider* will recall that after long and tortured negotiations, I was able to steal my 84 year old mother, Nancy, away from my brother Matthew's *Clinton Township McMansion* and got her to move in with me in Roseville. It was the free agent Signing of the Century, although I had to give up free rent, the parking spot in the garage next to the door, and an endless supply of bourbon and cokes.

Things were going fantastic Nancy in a great cook, and my wife, Roma, and mom love doing the crosswords together every day. My son, Liam, delights in making grandma her *Crystal Light* lemonades. Nancy even returned to painting after a 50 year hiatus, and would proudly show off her latest watercolors to any and all visitors, until my sister Jeannie's first attempt appeared to my mother to be superior to her own efforts. "I am disgusted," mom lamented. "Jeannie has never painted before and hers is already better than mine."

We tried to assure her, but she would not hear of it. She threatened to quit painting.

Then disaster struck. While driving north on Garfield at 15 Mile, she was sideswiped by a young man making a left turn. He got a ticket, but Nancy got two broken ribs, a lacerated spleen, and her car was totaled. We hoped to avoid surgery, and mom was out after a couple of days in the hospital. She was doing great, even painting, when suddenly after 10 days internal bleeding developed. That meant the spleen would have to go.

That was tough, and as they wheeled her away I feared I had seen the last of her. But she survived the surgery, no easy matter. As my sister Jeannie, a nurse (and blossoming painter) told Nancy as she lay in the recovery room, "Gee mom, you're kinda hard to kill."

Nancy is home now and gaining strength every day. Each of my 4 sisters came in turn from long distances to spend a week with her during her 2 hospital stays, often sleeping at the hospital. Ribs take a long time to heal, so Nancy will take it slow. But letters like the ones below from her grandchildren tend to cheer her up.

"*I just got off the phone with my mom, and she told me about your surgery. I am thinking about you, and I know you're going to be back in action soon because you're the toughest grandma around. You're like the Rahm Emanuel of grandmothers. I mean, it took a car accident to slow you down, and you're still truckin'. If I had my Law Degree, I would be out there in a flash to file a lawsuit against that jackass who rammed your car. What a dufus.*"

- Jeffrey

"*I'm thrilled that you're feeling better and back home. I hope these flowers will lighten up your living room and perhaps serve as inspiration for your next lovely watercolor (Jeannie's is crap). Keep getting better, don't let Mickey work you too hard, and I'll be back to visit soon. I love you.*"

- Nancy Helen

June 2010

A Funeral in Scotland

Death came suddenly to Janet Heaney. She had lived in Glasgow, Scotland for 90 years before passing quietly in an infirmary bed on December 29th. Her daughter Catherine, son-in-law Brian and grandchildren Christopher, Monica and Rosalind kept vigil.

Her youngest daughter, my wife Roma, answered the call the night before. Jenny had been given the last rites, Brian told her. She might not last the night, or she could hold on for a month. But Death was near. Roma, our son Liam, and I packed hurriedly and caught the next flight out of Detroit for Glasgow. Jenny died while we were in the air.

Janet McPhee was born in 1918, the 2nd of 6 children. She grew up in the rough and tumble of shipbuilding Glasgow, then the greatest city in the world. She worked in a Gentlemen's Outfitters store in the Gorbals, the toughest part of Glasgow, a job she loved and a community she cherished for the rest of her days.

She met her late husband Harry after a blind date was arranged over the phone. She hid in the house and instructed a friend to send him away if he had red hair. For his part, Harry gave her a false name until they had dated several times. They married during the war, and went on to have 5 children, including Gerald, a professional soccer player, Helena, the best constituent aide in Lansing, Robert, a surveyor, Catherine, a teacher, and Roma, a university administrator and Undefeated Debater at 31412 Gay Street.

These children and her 12 grandchildren were the focus of her life. Harry was a distinguished public official, working as a Rutherglen Town Councilor, Rent Officer, and Justice of the Peace. While he lived to serve others, Jenny lived to serve her family. With Harry away at meetings, Jenny cooked and cleaned and tried her best to control 5 rambunctious kids.

"I never got my highers," Jenny would always say, referring to her limited formal education, but she was nobody's fool. She was the hardest working person I have ever seen. When she'd come to America to visit, she used to clean the house all day, 24/7. Well into her 80s, she would clean our house spotless, and then take on major projects, like organizing all the canned goods in the pantry, or meticulously folding and arranging the linen closet.

No job was too big. It took the Good Lord 6 days to tame Leviathan and bring order to Chaos. But Jenny organized my basement and cleared out my garage in 2 days each, and with all due respect to the Almighty, her task was tougher, and she did a better job of it.

People used to try to lure her away from me, but neither I nor Liam would ever permit it. In Jenny's eyes, I could do no wrong. When I would come home from golfing, she would chastise Roma, saying "Michael, go lie down on the couch. You must be exhausted. Roma, get that poor boy a cup of tea." Jenny became a big high school basketball fan, thrilling to the spectacle of the halftime dance teams, and cheerleader acrobatics. She loved the stores in America. And she loved being with her grandson.

One time she came into Liam's room and sat contentedly watching him play his FIFA video soccer game for a good 10 minutes. The game is like Madden Football, complete with announcers and crowded noises and instant replays, and Liam was playing the big Glasgow Derby, Celtic against Rangers, Catholics against Protestants, which is a national event in Scotland.

Finally Jenny, thinking the game was real, said to Liam, "Why didn't you tell me the game was on?"

She was the most genuine, guileless person imaginable. How could you not love her?

She got the chance to meet Governor Granholm a few years ago at a bill signing ceremony in Lansing. "You are much more beautiful in person," she told the Governor, "and you are so much nicer than Mrs. Thatcher." For a moment Granholm forgot the pressures of being Governor, threw her head back, and laughed like she hadn't in years.

Jenny had been in declining health her last year. She began to suffer from dementia, and fell and broke her hip. She was recuperating in a nursing home, but Brian and Catherine and their 4 kids got her out and brought her to their home on Christmas Day. After initially protesting, she came along and was like the Jenny of old. She was sharp, and conversant, and they had a fantastic day together before taking her back in the evening.

During the night, Jenny fell ill, probably from an obstruction in her bowel. Too weak to survive an operation, her powerful heart finally gave out and she returned to the Lord on December 29th.

By coincidence, Jenny's brother-in-law Terry had passed without warning on Christmas Day, so we were able to attend his funeral also upon our arrival in Scotland. Jenny's funeral followed a few days later.

Brian did a great job organizing the funeral in the traditional Scottish way. We brought her body back to Brian and Catherine's house and visitors came to pay their respects and enjoy a cup of tea. We prayed the rosary there two nights, and then we carried the coffin, a plain wooden box, out of the house and took it to the church, leaving it in front of the altar overnight.

In the morning we celebrated the funeral, and Gerald and Brian gave fine eulogies to Jenny. We carried the coffin out on our shoulders again and then lowered it into the ground with ropes, in the same lair where Harry was buried 12 years ago. We each took handfuls of dirt and threw it on the casket. I will remember that image the rest of my days.

Jenny and Harry's dust will mingle together in the ground, and those left behind will remember both of them fondly. We concluded our affairs and prepared to return to Michigan. My brother Matthew called the night before our flight home with some welcome news. He and his wife are expecting their 3rd child this September. The sadness of Jenny's death was replaced with job for the coming of a new child.

The news would have pleased Jenny most of all.

May she Rest in Peace.

February 2009

People

The Rise and Fall of Kwame Kilpatrick

Unlike the vast majority of people who pass sweeping judgments on him, I actually know Kwame Kilpatrick. I served in the State House with him for 3 years before he was elected Mayor of Detroit.

Kwame is a complex person with many strengths and some tragic weaknesses. His Rise and Fall is a sad but all too familiar story in politics. How could a person who left the legislature mid-term in 2001 after a thrilling victory for Mayor a n r ii i i r i l, u i i o n beloved figure respected by both sides of the aisle, fall so fast and so hard to a man now serving 5 years in prison?

I first met Kwame Kilpatrick back in 1998. I had just won the Democratic Primary for an open State House seat. He called me because he was interested in running for Floor Leader, the number 2 ranking position among House Democrats. I suggested he meet me at St. Angela School in Roseville, where I would be picking up my son Liam from kindergarten.

I figured if he wanted to meet me, I would take the opportunity to show him where I come from and what I valued.

A natural politician, Kwame and Liam became fast friends. Although I didn't vote for him that first time, Kwame impressed me as a man of significant abilities who knew his way around the street. And in the greatest fiasco I've ever witnessed in politics, he won Floor Leader by one vote.

This was my welcome to Lansing. The 52 House Democrats met in the Capitol 2 days after the November Election of 1998. We had just lost the Majority in the House, and held a secret ballot for the 2 Minority Leadership positions.

Mike Hanley was elected Leader on the first ballot. After casting our votes for Floor Leader, a delegation of 3 members, including the chairman of the Caucus, went into an adjoining room to count the ballots. When they returned, the Caucus Chair declared Buzz Thomas the winner. Members leapt to their feet, clapping, cheering, pounding Buzz on the back and offering Kwame condolences.

I watched as Kwame, devastated, shook hands with Buzz.

Suddenly one member of the troika shouted, *"Wait! It's not Right!"*

A hush fell over the room.

"What do you mean?" Leader Hanley asked.

'"Its…that's not what the result was!"

You could have heard a pin drop. The Caucus was stunned. The delegation was ordered to go back to the room and recount the votes. They did and returned to report that Kwame had won by a single vote.

I can't imagine what it was like for the two of them, especially Buzz. He went from winner to loser, from elation to despair, in 2 minutes.

I thought the experience would teach Kwame a lifelong lesson in humility, having straddled the narrow line between winner and loser.

I guess it didn't.

Remember that I had just been elected 2 days before, and this was my first exposure to the Legislature. It was easily the worst meeting I've ever attended. To top it off, we re-elected the Caucus Chair by acclamation. That was like giving a "Good Government" award to the Florida Secretary of State for the 2000 Election.

I realized that first day I had entered an insane asylum. Two years later, I challenged the Caucus Chair and defeated him. He did not deserve to keep the job after screwing up the leadership election.

I watched Kwame in the job for those two years. Looking back, it was by far the worst session in my 10 years in the Legislature.

Republican Speaker Chuck Perricone (R-Kalamazoo Township) and Democratic Leader Michael Hanley (D-Saginaw) were sworn enemies and relations in the Chamber were awful. We made some historic blunders in policy, including unsupportable tax cuts that resulted in 8 years of deficits, and a Detroit School takeover that turned into a 5-year fiasco. We liquidated the Rainy Day Fund and the State plunged into debt.

Yet amid the chaos, Kwame demonstrated an ability to work with Republicans. His room for maneuver was limited, because he was only second in command. But he was one of the few Democrats able to shape policy rather than just oppose things.

When Hanley left thru term limits, Kwama came to see me about the leadership race at my district office in the Roseville Theatre Building. I backed him early and he appointed me to Appropriations, the most powerful and bi-partisan Committee in the Legislature.

In the 8 years since, I have risen to the top Democrat position, Minority Vice-Chair. In terms of my effectiveness, I regard this appointment as the key event in my legislative career.

Archer was still Mayor at the time of Kwame's visit, and his critics charged he was using Leadership as a stepping stone to launch a Mayoral race. I quizzed him on this. He claimed he had no plans to run and besides, Archer would be nearly impossible to beat. Though I had no knowledge of what was to happen, and was just guessing, I asked him what he would do if Archer didn't run.

He stopped for a second and peered at me through his narrowed eyelids.

"I'd have to take a look at that," he admitted quietly.

"I'd be disappointed in you if you didn't," I replied. I value ambition in a leader.

After Hanley left due to term limits, Kwame was able to do an outstanding job as Minority Leader in the House. He set the tone immediately at our Caucus retreat. The Republicans had elected a new Speaker, Rick Johnson (R-LeRoy), who was a collegial person and not a fire-eating partisan like Perricone.

"Things are going to be different this term," Kwame announced. "It's not all about gaining the Majority. You didn't come here to get the Republicans. You came here to help your constituents. From now on we won't judge everything in terms of winning the next election. Let's focus on doing good policy for the people we serve."

I can't stress enough to you how revolutionary this was. Kwame completely changed our orientation with these words. It was one of the most significant things anyone ever said to me about how to properly do my job.

For me, that was the high point of Kwame's career.

He later won a couple of tough races for Mayor, and did some good things to spur development in the City. But his accomplishments were dwarfed by some terrible abuses. Kwame is a big man with big appetites, and his desires got the better of him. I think he was too young at age 30 to realize he couldn't do as he pleased simply because he was the Mayor of Detroit. Kwame never seemed to understand this. He has no one to blame but himself.

He had too much power too early. He indulged his prodigious appetites and lacked the maturity and judgment to control his desires and became corrupt.

Were these faults always there? I suppose they were. But how could a man who saw public service with such clarity in 2000 become so blind and ethically lost just a few years later? It is a sad tale, both for him and for the City. Unlike many people I know, who seemed to relish in his failure, I took no joy in watching him self-destruct. It was an awful waste of talent and opportunity. It was a tragedy for the City and the Region. I pray his successors will not let power lead them into temptation, and so avoid a similar fate.

September 2008

On the Streets Where You Live

It's been 60 years since D-Day and the liberation of Europe. In honoring those who fought and died for us, it's instructive to reflect on how veterans shaped today's world.

My dad was an MP in WWII, and part of the invasion of Normandy in 1944 as a 23-year old kid. Like most veterans, he rarely talked about his experiences. But despite their reticence, yesterday's veterans have left an enduring mark, sometimes in subtle ways we hardly notice.

The greatest generation's victory over fascism transformed the world order. Their triumph led directly to the end of colonialism, the expansion of human and civil rights, and the establishment of American hegemony. The allied victory created the foundation for a peaceful and united Europe after two cataclysmic world wars only 21 years apart.

We take these gains for granted. We fail to appreciate, or even notice, how this world was even created. Reminders of our soldiers' contributions surround us, although few of us see the evidence in our daily lives. Yet if you only open your eyes and look closely, that half-forgotten world will come alive for you.

My awakening started one Memorial Day not so long ago. I'd just marched in the Roseville Memorial Day Parade as a Councilman. The ceremony culminated at City Hall with the High School band, a 21-gun salute, and the presentation of wreaths at the flagpole. As the crowd dispersed, I took a moment to look at the historical marker commemorating the war dead near the base of the flagpole.

As I read the names, I recognized a few to be street names in the city. Roseville boomed from rural Erin Township to a bustling suburb after the war. The city fathers and developers paid tribute to some of Roseville's slain heroes by naming streets after them. I felt enriched by knowing the background of the streets I trod so many times in blissful ignorance. I felt a better appreciation for the sacrifice and better grasped the debt and honor we owe to those vets.

The northwest corner of Roseville, East of Hayes and South of 13 Mile, is known as the only part of Roseville that's in the Fraser School District. But it should be known for something else, too. Just west of Dooley Elementary school is J. Carls Street.

J. Carls is famous locally as the home of Councilman John Chirkun. But few realize it was named for Jack William Carls, firecontrolman 3rd class of the US Navy. Jack survived 10 major naval engagements before losing his life in a typhoon in the south Pacific in December of 1944. He was only 22 and had graduated from Burton High and had worked for Bell Telephone before entering the service.

Just a short distance south from the Macomb Mall lies beautiful McKinnon Street, with its tall trees and huge 300-foot deep lots. Patton School is there, named after former principal Lucille Patton, no relation to US Army General George Patton. However, the Patton connection fits because the street itself is named for Corporal Jack Russell McKinnon, a 20-year old paratrooper who was killed in action in Italy on March 4, 1944. McKinnon was also a graduate of Burton, and made model airplanes as a kid before deciding to jump out of them for Uncle Sam. He had been overseas only 10 days when he was killed.

Jess Buckhannon grew up in the "Poets" district of Roseville on Ivanhoe Street, near Tennyson, Lowell, and Longfellow. An infantryman in the US Army, Jess died in November of 1944 in the South Pacific. His name appears on the tablets of the missing in Manila American Cemetery in the Philippines. He was honored with Buckhannon Street, half a mile southeast across Gratiot from his boyhood home.

Emery Street is well known to those who get lost trying to find a shortcut to 12 Mile from Roseville Junior High on Martin Road. But few realize that Wallace Emery was a Marine killed in a foxhole on Guam in the Pacific.

William Koontz likewise is commemorated with one of the longest streets in Roseville, stretching from 10 Mile near Kelly to I-696.

But Roseville's newest such eponymous street and most famous WWII causality is Wetzel Street in front of the City Hall, named for Macomb County's only Congressional Medal of Honor winner, Pfc. Walter C. Wetzel. He was killed in Germany when he threw himself on a hand grenade to save his fellow GIs.

These and many other veterans shaped our world. They created the fabric of our lives, from our freedom and independence down to the street where you live. Sometimes between the barbecues, and the sales, and the ballgames, take a moment to appreciate their sacrifice.

May 2004

A Tribute to Corporal Gentian Marku

"As you know, our colleague Senator Dennis Olshove (D-Warren) is home recuperating from illness. Therefore, I rise in his place to pay special tribute to U.S. Marine Corporal Gentian Marku, age 22, of Warren, Michigan, who was killed in action in Falluja, Iraq, on Thanksgiving Day.

Gentian was a recent immigrant to this country from his native Albania. When Gentian was 14, his future looked grim. Albania was in turmoil. The government collapsed amid scandals and bankruptcy. During the civil strife, military arsenals were looted by mobs. During the chaos, Gentian himself was skipping school often. When he did go, he got suspended for throwing an eraser at his teacher. Then his father won the U.S. State Department's Diversity Visa Lottery, a program that randomly selects foreign applicants for visas. The Marku family got the chance to immigrate to Warren, Michigan.

The move changed Gentian's life. "Everything changed when I got to the United States," he recalled. "I started studying. I got my first job ever as a busboy at Big Boy's. I stayed out of trouble." The story of the Marku family is a story that has been written millions of times in America. It is a story of immigrants coming to this country and working hard to build a new life. Gentian Marku's parents spoke little English and worked two and three jobs to give him and his young sister a chance for a good life.

Instead of pelting his teachers with erasers, Gentian spent extra hours with them in the Warren Woods/Tower ESL, that's the English as a Second Language program, learning to speak English. Luckily that was before many such programs were cut as a result of tight budgets. He handled the family bills and took care of things around the house, becoming a responsible adult while still a teenager.

I saw former Senator Art Miller (D-Warren) this morning. He knew Gentian and had seen him working as a busboy. He said to the owner of the restaurant, "Where did you get this kid? He does the work of three people. He is tremendous." Well, that is what Gentian was; he was a hard-working person.

He transformed himself into a high achieving, popular young man. He dreamed of being a Warren cop someday, so he joined the Explorers, a program for youngsters interested in careers as policemen. After graduation, he enlisted in the Marines, rising to the level of corporal. With his hard-won English skills, he served as the translator for the commander of the 26th Marine Expeditionary Unit during an official visit with Albanian civilian and military leaders.

He returned to his village. All of his relatives came to see him at his grandfather's house. They were impressed by the boy who had left his village six years earlier and had returned a man. "Six years ago," his Uncle Ndue announced, "a kid left Albania, and today a man stands before me who is part of the greatest military force in the world. I am happy he decided to join the Marines. It shows me he is very proud of the country where he now lives."

Gentian was killed on Thanksgiving Day in Falluja. Friends called it ironic because he was always thankful for the opportunities life offered when he came to America. Those opportunities come at a price. For us all to be free, a few pay a heavy price. Gentian's death was the price he paid so we all can enjoy a life of freedom and opportunity. As we work today to create a society that is better, fairer, and more just, I pray that we do it with a tenth of the bravery, commitment, and dedication to duty that characterized the life of Gentian Marku.

His family will return his body to the old country for burial with his ancestors. He will return there a U.S. citizen and a hero. America only had Gentian Marku for eight years. He enjoyed many opportunities from this country. America got much more in return from him. We, therefore, offer this tribute to the life of Gentian Marku and offer our heartfelt condolences to his family in this difficult time." (as quoted in the Journal of the Senate, December 2, 2004)

December 2004

Chillin' with Zvonko
Switalski and Haugh Open New District Office

Roseville's landmark bright green Theatre was built in 1929 at the historic Junction of Utica and Gratiot Avenue. I grew up going to the movies there for a quarter and getting my school shoes at the Roseville Department Store at the south corner of the building. I went to church and school across the street at Sacred Heart. After college, I worked for Russ LaBarge's Law Firm in the north end of the Theatre Building. I still get my hair cut at Bob the Barber's, in the middle of the building, where Bob Slain has been cutting hair over 50 years.

I have great affection for the Theatre, and I maintained my district office there for 10 years. But it was time to move. My suite mate, former Representative Frank Accavitti, was term-limited and was moving out. My friend Harold Haugh was elected to replace him, and we agreed to take a fresh look at what was available in our districts.

The Theatre had great character and location, which I often stressed to Zvonko Blazevski, my long suffering Aide who mans the District Office. Zvonko is a very dedicated worker. He comes early and stays late. He is hyper, with an abundance of energy. He is always doing 3 things at once, which he calls multitasking. He's even going to school for his mater's degree at night.

Nevertheless, he would listen patiently to tales of my first cigarette in the Theatre bathroom with Ricky Scarcella, or a kiss stolen from Patty Saputo, the Beauty of Biehl Street.

Then he would interject more practical concerns, point to the ice forming inside the spacious windows, or the birds nest bits strewn on the inside sills. He would make it a point to call me each time the toilet backed up. Zvonko turned a deaf ear to my entreaties to empty the trash daily, because he is devoted to St. Francis, and was on a mission to provide for the occasional mouse.

All these indignities he would have suffered gladly, but for one last hardship. Although the high tin ceiling was beautiful, and the enormous windows offered great urban vistas of the Junction and Gonzo's mural, they contributed to Baltic temperatures in the office.

We had a thousand more square feet than we really needed. The furnace ran constantly, but it was undersized. Despite being the little furnace that couldn't, the heating bill approached $1000 a month, and Zvonko still shivered. I tried insulation and weather stripping, to little effect. Every time he plugged in the space heater he blew a fuse. I'm not saying it was cold, but I walked in one morning, and saw sides of beef hanging from the ceiling, and Zvonko was warming his McGriddles by placing them inside the refrigerator.

As a concerned boss, I told him to put on another coat. My distress heightened when, despite fingerless gloves, the typing speed of his frozen digits plummeted and the email response backlog rose inversely with the temperature.

"Don't worry, Zvonko," I reassured him, as I aimed a blow dryer at his hands. "Spring will be here before you know it."

But Spring led to the Scourge of Summer. Without air conditioning, the office sweltered. I urged Zvonko to dress for the weather, but he is a first generation immigrant, old school. He wears shirt and tie, and dress pants, and argued that a speedo was inappropriate for the office. That eliminated the option of setting up a hose and sprinkler for him to run thru during his breaks.

Although Zvonko's comfort weighed chiefly on my mind, I reviewed my office budget, which had been trimmed annually in these tough times. Summer brought no utility respite. What I saved on the gas furnace, I paid in electricity, because Zvonko ran about 5 fans in order to maintain consciousness. He refused to open the doors for cross ventilation, because the traffic noise distracted him.

The return of winter spelled misery for Zvonko. With reluctance, I decided I must liberate him from Siberia. Harold and I looked around and found a great new location on Gratiot just north of 13 Mile Road, just south of Sajo's Restaurant and north of the Shadowoods Sunoco gas station. The square footage is smaller and the furnace larger, so it is cozy. We even saved a little on rent. After some renovations, Zvonko settled in, and I am happy to report the feeling has returned to most of his fingers.

Now all I have to do is get him to empty the garbage, which is always full of empty Red Bull cans.

Maybe that's why he is so jumpy. I'd better put the heat on low and slow him down.

February 2009

Marge Notte 1946—2004

First Lady of Sterling Heights

Marge Notte, the wife of Sterling Heights Mayor Richard Notte, died July 2nd after fighting valiantly against cancer since December. She was 58 years old. Marge was a loving wife, mother, and grandmother, a good friend, a great sister, and a significant influence on all she encountered.

I got to know Marge only a few years ago, but my wife Roma and I always enjoyed her company. She was straightforward in her dealings, with a biting wit and sharp tongue. If Marge didn't like what you did, she'd tell you to your face. And she was a lot of fun to be around, as her collection of girlfriends, the Golden Girls, could attest to. I suspect the Golden Girls, a sort of Ya-Ya Sisterhood that included Judge Kim Wiegand, Chamber of Commerce head Lil Adams, and Sterling Heights Community Relations Director Pat Lehman, could tell some wild tales if they wanted. Instead they set up a women's charity in Marge's honor.

Marge was a woman of considerable political skill. I remember sitting in her kitchen one evening and eavesdropping on a conversation she was having with one of the Sterling Heights "Redshirt" residents bitterly opposed to the noise from Freedom Hill Park. Mayor Notte and the Council had taken their side and fought to protect the residents, but the court case was not going well.

Many politicians would have stressed how hard they were fighting for the residents, blamed the judge or claimed corruption. They would have taken the easy way out by putting themselves in the best light, everyone else in the worst, and telling the resident what he or she wanted to hear.

But Marge was tougher and more honest than that.

She told the resident that the council believed in the justice of the case, but that it owed a responsibility to all the other residents of the city, too. The council had to balance the escalating cost and reduced probability of success in the fight to determine what would be a fair resolution. Marge never manipulated constituents but rather always worked to educate and lead.

She was an invaluable political asset to her husband, offering sagacious advice and great organizational skills. "You know, it's always we women who do all the work," she pointed out to me during one campaign. "You men just get all the credit." Although I find Dick incredibly organized, Marge maintained that men were generally poorly organized beings. She used to look at me when she said that.

She and Dick were a great match. It was the second marriage for both of them, and they shared incredible inner strength. Sadly, they needed it, as Dick lost a child of his first marriage and Marge and Dick's daughter, Annie, died tragically in a train accident.

But they endured, even giving birthday parties for Annie in the years after she died. These parties weren't maudlin affairs, but celebrations. All Annie's friends came.

Dick and I were sitting in the Sterling Heights Library, holding our office hours one night, when he received a panicky call from Marge. She had lost control of her arm, which was flailing, and she was shaken and needed to see a doctor. Dick left immediately. Marge was soon diagnosed with lung and brain cancer in its late stages. In a courageous decision characteristic of her, Marge decided to forego aggressive chemotherapy and radiation treatments in the hope of living her remaining days more fully.

I visited Marge during this time and she was a marvel. She was matter-of-fact about her condition and realistic about her prospects, yet she had things she wanted to do. Our conversations never centered on her or her illness. She lived far longer than the doctors predicted. During her illness, she and Dick sold their house and bought a condominium. She was determined to live long enough to move into the new condo and to get Dick settled and properly organized.

The day they moved in, Marge was fully engaged, directing the movers and making sure the house was set up right. By all accounts, she did a great job. It must have been exhausting. Marge had met her goal, successfully concluding her bargain with cancer on her own terms. The day after the move, Marge lapsed into a coma, dying several days later.

At the funeral mass, Lil Adams read from the apostle Paul's letter to Timothy:

"The hour of my dissolution is at hand, for I am already being poured out as a drink offering. I have fought the good fight, I have finished the race, I have kept the faith."

I sat with Councilwoman Barb Ziarko at the funeral luncheon. Barb saw to it that everyone at the table was served Marge's favorite drink, vodka and orange, no ice, and led a toast to her, announcing, "This drink shall here forward be known as the Marge Notte."

You led a good life.

Here's to ya, Marge.

July 2004

Katrina: Desperately Seeking Survivors

I went to Louisiana State University in Baton Rouge, about 60 miles from New Orleans, so when Katrina hit, I was worried about some of my college pals. Most of my buddies have moved away since I left Louisiana in 1981, either to Texas, Ohio, California, or Washington. But I had a couple of old girlfriends who were still in the path of the hurricane, and I got very uneasy.

It's one thing to read or hear about people, or even to see them on TV suffering and dying. But to have people you have known and loved be missing in harm's way can be very unsettling. I hadn't spoken to one of these women in 23 years, but after Katrina I was on the computer and telephone all day trying to track down these women's whereabouts.

I called my friends and asked them to help me look for them, and I checked *The List* created by the Red Cross to see if I could find their names or any of their family's names. I googled them. I got out my LSU Alumni Directory and looked up their employers. But neither of them were on *The List* because you have to put yourself on the list, and if your house has washed away and you are living out of your car or wading thru the street or worse, the last thing you have on your mind is finding a secure internet connection.

All these things went thru my mind as I made my search, but the thoughts were not comforting. I finally found them safe and secure after a week, and I felt like I had won the lottery. I talked to them both by email, heard their stories, and felt so happy that they were alive. But I felt like a rotten friend who had neglected to stay in touch with them for so long. I thanked God for giving me a second chance to be a better friend and a better person.

Gaynell was living in Belle Chasse, south of New Orleans right on the Mississippi and directly in Katrina's path. The *New York Times* had printed a map one day with a big circle around Belle Chasse which had put me in a panic. But she told me that her whole extended family, including her kids, her parents, her sister's family and brother's family, had all evacuated early Sunday to beat the traffic and were in a motel room in Northwest Louisiana. She is a grade school teacher and who knows what will happen to Belle Chasse. She tells me everything on the south side of the town is gone.

Her biggest concern was her brother, who was a New Orleans cop and whom they hadn't heard from for nearly a week. He was finally given three days R&R and they were all so thankful he was OK. Tynia was safe in New Jersey, but likewise had a brother on the New Orleans fire department who had some stories to tell.

I asked what I could do for them, but Southerners, and especially Southern Women, are incredibly strong and proud people. They are very gracious people. I know when they get back to their homes and families and survey the damage, that they will resolutely rebuild their lives.

They will tell colorful stories for generations about the terrible events of these last weeks. I learned at LSU what a great part of the country the South is, the only part of America to taste defeat in war and to be occupied. Adversity builds character, and New Orleans of all places is full of characters.

I have no doubt the South shall rise again.

September 2005

Ashley Morris Wins Rosenthal Award
Recognized as Best Intern in the Michigan Legislature

Daniel Rosenthal was a promising student intern in the Capitol in 1977 but passed away in June of that year. As a memorial, his family established thru MSU an annual award to honor the top student intern in Lansing. Congressman Vern Ehlers established an additional award for the runner up. These awards recognize and honor the valuable work of all interns, and both awards include a cash stipend.

I have had some outstanding interns over the last 12 years, including Irene Kepler, who was a Rosenthal Award winner and went on to become a Roseville City Councilwoman and a Macomb County Commissioner. But without disparaging the quality work done by many fine interns who have worked faithfully for me, Ashley Morris is, by far, the finest intern I have ever had, and is one of the most remarkable people I have ever known. If she had worked for me 10 years ago, I would probably be Governor by now.

Ashley is in her second year of law school at MSU, so she has an advantage in age and experience over most undergraduate interns. But that isn't what makes her unique. She is very bright, and articulate. But it isn't that either. Intelligence is a great asset, but Ashley brings something to the job that trumps pure smarts.

She listens, closely. She questions, pointedly, until she understands the problem or issue, and then she fearlessly and relentlessly gets the answer to that problem. She does this rapidly, and then reports the answer or proposed resolution, succinctly, and can answer any question on the process and also lays out other, less preferred, options.

What is most impressive about her ability to do this is that the subject can be something she knows nothing about. But her intellectual fearlessness kicks in, and she tackles and masters the essentials of the issue, and moves toward a solution.

I had long been dissatisfied with my website, both its design, and my use of it. I have muddled through with it for 7 years in the Senate, but I was unable to articulate a vision of what it should be, or how I should use it. As I have over the years with several other people, I asked Ashley to take a look at it and tell me what she thought of it, and what I should do with it.

Two days later she came to me and pointed out some obvious flaws. It was not user friendly, and wasn't updated often. I asked her what she recommended. She told me she had looked at every other Democratic Senator's site, and there were 3 that were doing interesting things. She showed me the 3, leading up to the one she thought was good. She proposed copying that site, and remaking mine in its image. I liked what I saw. She offered to review the 22 other Republican sites, but I had seen enough. Her proposal worked.

Ashley then proceeded, never having done web design before, to redo the entire site, incorporating changes I suggested along the way. She did this by following technical instructions on the site itself, which I have absolutely no patience for and could never do. And she did it at virtually no cost, which I love, and in record time.

I was astonished.

I immediately turned her loose on my e-newsletter. I put a lot of effort into it, updating my blog every 2 weeks, but the newsletter was a sprawling mess, too long for the typical online reader. I asked her the same questions as I had about the website, but this time I was more direct. "It's garbage, isn't it?" I asked.

Most employees, let alone an intern, wouldn't have the guts to pass judgment on their boss's own work product. I was waiting to see how she would handle this.

"Anything can be improved," she responded, matter of factly.

I thought about that answer for days. I still think about it. She told me it was lousy, but she did it with the tact of a seasoned diplomat. Instead of passing judgment on the format, she changed the question and simply made the indisputable observation that we could make the newsletter better. I would never have thought of answering the question that way. And I have been in politics for 20 years!

The newsletter is now 2 pages long, and half of it is interactive letters from constituents. But even this will be improved and reimagined.

At this point I decided I was underutilizing Ashley's talents. I considered sending her to the Middle East, to resolve the centuries old conflicts there. But since she had another year of law school to complete, I asked her to evaluate a complicated tax reform and revenue proposal I am secretly hatching.

I wanted to know if my theory justifying the tax is consistent with the tax's actual provisions. She had tax codes and papers spread out over a desk and two tables for several days, and she had a lot of fun with it. She helped me present it to the Budget Director one day, and to the Treasurer a bit later. She played her supporting role perfectly, providing technical information when called upon.

I see Ashley as my equal, and we went toe to toe debating the merits of a controversial vote regarding rescinding state employee pay raises. There aren't many people, even legislators, who you can have an honest argument with, keep to the issues, and not let the argument get personal. That's unfortunate, because it is the best way to make good decisions. The debate was so good I insisted on renewing it 2 days later when Ashley returned to work. In the end, we agreed to disagree. But we had an appreciation, and respect, for each other's reasoning.

You have to be careful when arguing with Ashley. She has a persistent habit of talking to you, even looking at you, while she is looking up the answer to the question you are debating online. She can do this with stunning speed. I am blessed with a great Chief of Staff, Jeff Minore, and sometimes when he and I are trying to make sense of some missing data or vague policy issue, Ashley will interject the key information or definition from her quick search.

I believe I was the bigger beneficiary when Ashley came to work in my office, but her application to the Rosenthal Committee detailed some of the benefits she received. Ashley wrote that "what I will carry with me when I leave this office are things I couldn't read in books or find online. Sure, learning to research more efficiently is a strength for any law student or attorney, and writing memos and preparing presentations is essential. These skills only scratch the surface of what I have gained from my experiences though. I learned the value of knowledge, the importance of educating myself enough to have my own opinion, rather than following whatever is mainstream at the moment. I found that not only did I have a voice, but if I had an understanding of what I wanted to talk about, people would truly listen to what I had to say."

I recently gave Ashley a major bill I sponsored to reform the Detroit Pension System. I have never done this before with an issue this controversial. I generally keep such bills to myself, but in this case I believe she will help me gain passage. Last week, sessions ran long and I was going to miss a big meeting I set up with some Michigan Employee Retirement System executives. I told Ashley she would have to handle the meeting alone, and that she had to ensure she was taken seriously and not dismissed as "just an intern."

I don't know why I even bothered to say that. With Ashley Morris, that quite simply could never happen.

April 2010

The Campaign Trail

It's a Family Affair

All politics are local. And nothing's more local than your own family. For better or worse, several of my family members have turned to politics as a career. Call it civic duty, selfless altruism, or just plain lust for power and glory, in my book nothing beats politics for its fascinating characters, relevance, and opportunity to make a difference in the world.

I guess it was my mother, Nancy Ann Switalski, who got us all started. She was the first person in my family ever to serve in public office. She was appointed to a vacancy on the Roseville City Council. She served with distinction and integrity and was promptly beaten at the next election.

That was my family's first real lesson in politics. It's a rough, highly competitive game. My ma has a lot of great attributes. But if you want to succeed in politics, you need more than beauty, charm, intelligence, and good intentions.

You need to campaign hard.

By the time my older brother Mark decided to run for District Judge more than a decade later, he'd figured out how to do that. He built his campaign around an organizing principal of family and friends. He and I knocked doors on opposite sides of the street together throughout the district—the cheapest and most effective campaign tactic. We got our family and friends to deliver literature house to house. We worked harder than we had at anything we've ever done. And he won big.

My little brother Matthew is now running for Judge. He's been an attorney for 7 years and a prosecutor for Macomb County for the last 4 years. He's won some impressive convictions in the Circuit Court. He'll work hard to build on what has become a family tradition.

Some people question the appropriateness of having 3 brothers serving in government.

It's a legitimate question.

I won't flatter us by mentioning us in the company of the Kennedys, the Bushes, or the Hertels, who have all done pretty well.

I just look at it this way. My Dad had a family business. He sold tombstones for *Sheldon Granite* at 8 Mile and Woodward in

Detroit. He was the first kid in his family to finish high school. He stressed to us kids the importance of getting an education. But he didn't pay for our college. His greatest gift to me and my brothers was to give us *a job*. He taught us to value hard work and built in us a determination to succeed. My brothers and I all worked like dogs in the *Sheldon* shop, carving stones and monuments to work our way through college.

My dad died at 58 and *Sheldon's* is long gone. We boys have transformed that family business with the values my parents taught us. Values of hard work and integrity. And the new family business is *Politics*.

Some people criticize this family connection. But a good name is everything in politics. Corporations work hard to earn consumers' trust in their brand name or product. Politicians work just as hard to build that same type of confidence in their names. Isn't that a good thing?

My family knows that if any one of us screws up, the *Switalski* name is on the line. We've worked hard to build a reputation for honesty and fairness, and try not to do or say anything we'd be ashamed to see in the paper the next day. A good name is a burden. But it is a burden well worth bearing.

I've relied on my family for a lot of help. My sister-in-law Helena Heaney works for me in Lansing. I believe she is the best constituent worker in the whole legislature. She takes a personal interest in my constituents and their problems and works tirelessly to right wrongs. She is a bureaucrat's worst nightmare, and the best friend of a sympathetic public servant. I talked her into quitting her job in Louisville, moving to Lansing and working for me at a big pay cut. She does it because of her sense of social mission, a desire to help people with problems, and to help me. She is the best thing I've done in 4 years in the Legislature.

I'm lucky to have a family who supports me. My wife Roma puts up with my foibles and my frequent absences while I'm in Lansing. My 9-year old son Liam gets up on occasion and drops literature with me. I am blessed with many nieces and nephews who are helping me. My 23-year old nephew Neil McKenna has come here from Glasgow, Scotland to help me campaign all year. As soon as school ends in Baltimore, my 9th grade nephew Andrew Krebs will join us, together with my 24-year old niece

Nancy Van der Veer, an all-state volleyball player and future Senator from Rhode Island.

My house will resemble a bunkhouse before this campaign is over. But this is my opportunity to teach the next generation of my family, be they McKennas, Van der Veers, Krebs, or Switalskis. This is my chance to convey the lessons of loyalty and sacrifice and work that my parents taught me so well.

These kids make me proud.

And their help shows me they've already learned these lessons.

April 2002

Life in the Bunkhouse

When I decided to run for the Senate I knew I would need the considerable support of my family and friends. I prefer to distribute this newsletter you're reading by hand. It's cheaper than mailing it and I get to know the neighborhoods, which is what I should be doing if I want to represent the area. Since the Senate district is 270,000 people, I can't physically drop the whole thing each month. So I alternate mailing half the district and hand delivering the other half each month.

My crew of family and friends goes out at the crack of dawn every morning doing this. I've convinced two of my nephews, **Neil McKenna** of Glasgow, Scotland and **Andrew Krebs** of Baltimore, and my niece **Nancy Helen VanderVeer**, of Arizona by way of Rhode Island, to move into my house and go out with me and my friends each morning.

Thank God for bunk beds. And these young adults bring a vitality to the household. Sometimes it's like an episode of MTV's *The Real World*.

Neil completed his degree last year in Pharmacology at Glasgow University, and is now conducting clinical trials on the respective absorption rates for Cloverleaf and Pappy's Pizza by the human digestive system. He has found some willing guinea pigs in the bunkhouse, or as Liam calls it, the *gross room*.

Niece Nancy is an athletic blonde graduate of Smith College. She joined the Teach America program and taught 6th grade for two years in a disadvantaged area in Arizona. She is applying to Law Schools now and I believe will use the knowledge she learns on this campaign to someday be elected Senator from Rhode Island.

Andrew just got all A's at St. Joseph High School in Baltimore. The lacrosse team is floundering without him, but he is inquisitive and hard working and a big asset to my campaign.

Assembling this crack team wasn't easy.

My wife Roma and I schemed over how to recruit our kin. I worried that the thrill of helping me on my campaign might not be sufficient motivation to entice my relations to give up a summer of video games, malls, beaches and generally goofing off in exchange for a daily 5 am lit drop. Finally I emerged from the situation room.

"I've got it!" I shouted. "We buy an old Miata, and then we say 'I really need your help on his campaign, and gee, we got this car for you to drive while you're here. Is it acceptable?'"

Roma enthusiastically endorsed the idea, so I shopped around on *AutoTrader.com* and got a white convertible with 100,000 miles on it for under $5000.

"That was an inspired stroke of genius," observed my wife, as my youthful kin lined up to volunteer for the following summer's campaign.

"Now you understand I'll have to take it out every so often just to keep the battery up," I warned Roma.

"What an inconvenience," Roma fretted. "I suppose it's a price you'll have to pay."

"I'm willing to make the sacrifice," I offered nobly. "But also, intermittent periods of inactivity will also lead to the buildup of performance-reducing carbon in the engine," I continued. "I'm afraid I will be forced to drive it occasionally at high rates of speed to maintain vehicular quality."

"It's your solemn duty to the children," she reassured me.

I returned home recently to find 15-year old Andrew in the driver's seat, parked in the garage, probably fantasizing about Highway 101 in California.

Mission accomplished.

A political campaign tests your management skills. It requires the ability to recruit, motivate, and direct many volunteers. Lots of friends have helped me. And these kids are out with me every morning, 7 days a week. I'm not saying I work these kids hard, but the term "slavedriver" has come up on occasion. When the kids are exhausted and need a break, I arrange for them to go work in a salt mine for a week to recover.

We generally start at 5 am and eat breakfast after the drop at about 9:30 am, and then the kids fall in a heap and take a nap. The heat and grinding work hasn't dulled Neil's wry Scottish wit. As he staggered off to collapse on the couch, he summoned my 9-year old son Liam. "Don't waken me," he ordered, "unless the Germans are advancing on Roseville."

With big signs, and lawnsigns, and literature to print and fold and mailings to prepare, there is always plenty to do. And with troops like these, I can't go wrong.

August 2002

The Education of Liam Switalski

I am the son of the late, great Norbert Switalski. And the apple does not fall far from the tree. All fathers share a magnificent obsession. I am no different from my father before me.

And I am certain that someday my son Liam will join this quest long after I am gone. This mission is fundamental to the success of the human enterprise. It is more important than any other job men do in life.

We must teach our sons the value of work.

My father was devoted to this duty. He preached his sermon of hard work to me and my brother Mark constantly, and in many ways. He was at work on my younger brother Matthew when he died suddenly at age 58. One reason he went into the tombstone business was to provide jobs for me and my brothers and sisters. He wanted us to work hard, do a good job, and take pride in what we made.

Like most kids, we resisted these lessons. I remember many lazy summer afternoons, lying on the couch with my brother, watching some ball game, while my dad was out in the backyard mowing the lawn.

Now I am the one mowing the lawn.

Except my son isn't watching the Tigers. He's playing video games with his cousins. Like my father, I devote much of my time and energy to plotting over how to indoctrinate my son.

The most common method of nagging, ordering or otherwise imposing work, is ineffective. To be truly successful, the student has to believe *within himself* that work is what gives life meaning. You can't impose that by issuing orders. You have to unlock the mind and change the heart. The second method, bribery, is more effective, but it is expensive. It promotes avarice rather than appreciation for work. Nevertheless, I tried this for years on my son. I attempted to bargain his allowance in return for certain chores.

He turned me down at an early age. "I have no use for money," he said dismissively.

I suppose I could have withheld meals and shelter, but there was something about his attitude, and the beauty and simplicity of this phrase, that I had to admire. My approach would have to become more sophisticated.

His grade school years went by, and he was an excellent student, well-behaved, and excelled at basketball and soccer. My wife and I feel lucky to have such a fine son. But still I plotted secretly on how to accomplish my sacred mission.

I was reduced to everyone's least favorite option: teaching by example. Though effective, this method has the unfortunate side effect of forcing you to work hard yourself all the time. And hope the lesson is absorbed through osmosis.

Then, without warning, it happened. A miracle occurred.

Liam was dropping literature with me and his cousins Andrew and Sebastian for our cousin Jon, who is running for an open seat in the House of Representatives. We get up early, about 5:30 in the morning, and walk thru the neighborhoods putting Jon's campaign literature on people's doors. It is hard work, but we save Jon 42 cents with every house we do. And he doesn't owe anyone anything for getting elected, other than volunteers who want him to do a good job.

Jon is like the perfect father. He sets the example by working the hardest of us all. He drops lit in the morning, works his job for the Service Employees International Union all day, and then knocks on people's doors and introduces himself at night.

We've been doing the morning lit drops since April, and one day Liam was dropping a condominium. He was stopped by a representative of the homeowners association, who said there was no soliciting.

"I am not soliciting," Liam said. "This is campaign literature."

"You can't deliver that, either."

"But my cousin has a court case that says we can," Liam protested.

"We don't care about that." Reluctantly, Liam stopped.

The rest of the weekend, he must have complained to my wife, Roma, and me 50 times a day that his 1st Amendment rights to free speech had been violated. His freedom had been curtailed. Life wasn't the same for him after this grave injustice.

I had my staff pull together the legal background to the issues of soliciting, private property restrictions, and related matters. It's actually quite interesting. And this 15-year old is very interested.

A short time later Jon asked if he wanted to try knocking doors, and Liam agreed. He did it, and he was good at it.

"He was a novice," recalled John, "but he learned quickly. He excelled in connecting with total strangers. And I was amazed at his lack of shyness."

For the rest of the summer, Liam's typical day started with a lit drop from 6:00 to 9:00 am, soccer practice from 9:30 till 11:30, put up some signs or play (video games) with his cousin, and then knock doors from 5 pm till 8 pm.

He did this all without complaint.

And he did it every day.

Liam has become a man.

September 2008

Isn't It Time For a Change?

My name is Mickey Switalski and I am running for Congress. It isn't easy to take on a 28-year incumbent. But I don't like the way things are going, and I think I can do a better job.

That's the key.

We can't keep doing things the same way and expect different results. This is the worst economy in 70 years, and we have to be willing to make changes. We need new leadership and a more energetic approach to our problems.

It comes down to this.

I think I can do a better job.

So now I *have* to run.

If I think I can do a better job, it would be cowardly and unpatriotic *not to run*.

Party regulars have tried to talk me out of running. Some have told me I can't win, I am crazy for doing this, and that I will be outspent 100 to 1. Except for the "can't win" part, most of those things are probably true. But I like being outspent 100 to 1.

It proves I am fiscally conservative.

Some suggest that by running against a long-time incumbent, I am being disloyal. But our democratic system wasn't created to make *politician's* lives more comfortable. Democracy thrives on competition. If we treat incumbency like it's an *entitlement*, we deserve to get bad representation.

I am providing a public service by running. I am giving people the most valuable thing there is in life: *a choice*. What good are elections if you don't get to make an actual choice?

Some people like to denigrate me by saying I am only running because I am term-limited. I *am* term limited. But from my point of view, we are *all* term limited. At the end of every term you get to pick your representative. No one is *guaranteed* a job in politics. Holding office is a job you have to *earn* every day. When you start taking it for granted, you should be replaced.

When my term ends December 31, 2010, I will have been in politics for 22 years. I served as a City Councilman, County Commissioner, State Rep and now Senator.

It's been a good run. But I also worked in the private sector. For almost 10 years I worked for General Dynamics in Labor

Relations at the Detroit Arsenal Tank Plant. So I have a chance now to do something new. But I am *choosing* to run for Congress. It would be a lot easier to choose something else. I wouldn't have to get up at 5 am everyday and stick this newsletter in your door.

I am running because I have something to offer. And it is needed.

So what kind of Congressman would I be?

Similar to the kind of Senator I've been.

I have tried to be bi-partisan in the Michigan Senate. I have worked closely with colleagues on the other side of the aisle to fix problems and get results for my constituents. I have taken many unpopular positions on controversial issues, when I thought they were right. I figured you would respect someone who told you unpleasant truths a lot more than someone who tells you what he thinks you want to hear.

We could use that right now.

I believe Democrats should be the party of the working people. We should stand for just that–*hard work*. I think I can only earn your respect by working harder for you than anyone else out there. I have worked hard and gotten results in the Senate. I introduced more legislation than any other senator last session, and the session before that, for that matter.

I also passed more bills into law, by a long shot, than any other Democrat. I was second in the prior session. The only Senate Democrat who passed more was Bob Emerson, the Minority Leader, who is now the State Budget Director.

I am the ranking Democrat on the most powerful committee in the legislature, the Appropriations Committee. I sponsored some major legislation, like the early collection of County Millage a few years ago, which saved the state $200 million a year and protected Revenue Sharing for Counties for a decade.

It was controversial. But it was right.

I have the guts to do the tough cuts that we are making in state government right now. I represented the Senate Democrats in recent negotiations over Executive Order cuts that slashed over $300 million in spending. The cuts were tough. They resulted in the first layoffs of state employees in living memory.

But it's nothing my constituents haven't experienced. And they rightfully expect government to take the same medicine that they swallow. Government can't be exempt from our common economic pain.

We have huge issues over debt and budget deficits in Washington. I could help here. Some of my most significant contributions in Lansing dealt with budget issues.

I was at the center of the negotiations to resolve the budget crisis of 2007 when we had a brief shutdown of state government. I pushed for a balanced compromise of cuts, taxes, and reforms that was finally adopted. I was one of only two Democrats in the Senate to make the tough votes to fix our problems in the wee hours of October 2007. I voted to restore taxes to their 2000 level, a hard vote most Republicans avoided, and voted for the reforms of public employee pension and health care, a tough vote most Democrats avoided. The only other Democrat to cast both of these tough votes was the Senate Minority Leader, Mark Schauer.

And he is now a Congressman.

To me, that is the test of leadership. Everyone talks the talk about bipartisanship, but I actually walk the walk. I cast the votes that made these things pass. These are tough votes because you end up angering people on both sides of the political spectrum. But there were the essence of the compromise because both sides got, and gave up, something. And when they passed by one vote, mine was the deciding vote.

I hope you want someone who will solve our problems, not someone who will play to your prejudices. When people get 90+ percent liberal or conservative voting records, they are not getting their hands dirty making the tough choices to advance policy.

They are just safely voting their ideology and blaming the other side.

You deserve better than that.

I am making these tough calls right now. With the economic crisis, it is necessary to make cuts to state spending and to change the way we offer government services. We can't afford to do things the way we've been doing them. Without a healthy Chrysler and GM, we don't have the same level of resources. I have sponsored reform legislation that will consolidate elections to one a year in November, eliminate wasteful spending on MEAP testing in schools by privatizing the tests, and stop double dipping retirement bonuses that discourage retirement at a time we are laying off employees.

One of my proudest days in the Senate came one morning after several weeks of gridlock over the cigarette tax. The legislature had agreed to raise the cigarette tax, but we had been arguing for weeks over whether the money should be dedicated to Medicaid or go into the General Fund. Every week we failed to reach an agreement, we lost money from not raising the cigarette tax. As we repeated the same sterile debate for the umpteenth time, I went to the podium.

I suggested what I thought would be a fair compromise. I said we should put the money the first year into Medicaid, where we had a deficit, and thereafter put it into the General Fund, where the legislature could allocate it annually according to its priorities.

The Senate Majority Leader, Republican Ken Sikkema, got up immediately, God love him, and said, "You know what? I never thought of doing it that way."

Within half an hour we had an agreement and passed the tax. Lieutenant Governor John Cherry, who is the Presiding Officer of the Senate, came down from the rostrum. "Mickey," he said to me, "You just saved everybody's summer vacation!"

That was a great day to me, because I felt I had done my job. I listened to both sides and suggested a solution. Others were open-minded enough to listen and adopt it. Government worked.

I pledge to you that I will get results, resolve disputes, and fix problems if you put me in Congress. I think we need a lot less partisanship and a lot more pragmatism from our government.

I would appreciate your support.

I better admit to you right now that I am cheap.

I pride myself on running cheap campaigns, and that starts with this newsletter. I write, print and distribute it myself, with as many friends helping me as I can convince. We get up early, about 5 am, and stick it in your door handle. Throughout the course of this campaign I expect I will be on your porch half a dozen times, or at least across the street from you. It's exhausting, but I get a fantastic education on conditions in your neighborhood, what the problems are, what the foreclosures are like, and the quality of city services. I get a sense of the spirit of the area and of the city. I think I ought to know these things if I aspire to represent you.

I won't see many of you at that hour, but later in the day I hope to knock on your door and meet you. I hope you like what you see. I do this partly because I want to show you that I will work hard. And I want to demonstrate to you, the best way I know how, that I am just like you. I come out of the same type of neighborhood and share the same background and face the same challenges.

If you like the way things are going you can vote to put the same people back in office. I think it is time for change and some different approaches. I will bring new energy to the office that is long overdue.

I hope you will consider me.

September 2009

Senator Switalski, I charge you with cooperating with Republicans...

How do you plead?

"GUILTY"

Mickey, how many times do I have to tell you? "Bipartisan" is just something you're supposed to say, not something you're supposed to do!

A New Kind of Democrat

I am a new kind of Democrat. I am a Democrat that values *Fiscal Responsibility*, which means paying your bills, reducing your debt, and putting away something for a rainy day. It means bringing your expenses in line with your revenues.

Fiscal Responsibility requires only one rule. If your idea costs money, pay for it.

Unfortunately, both parties violate this rule. Even my *fiscally conservative* Republican friends.

Republicans preach responsibility, but they often stumble in practice. They will cut spending, except for programs *they* like. This year they wanted to spend more on Prisons, State Police, and Agriculture than the Democrats. They only let me cut one judge in Macomb when nearly everyone wanted to cut two.

They have been disappointing on Government Consolidation. The State has 16 Departments. The Governor wants eight, and I support her.

But my Republican friends have challenged her elimination of the Department of History Arts and Libraries. She combined the Departments of Environmental Quality and Natural Resources, and wanted to add in Agriculture, but they watered down her initiative. If they really want to save money, Republicans should be *pushing* instead of *impeding* consolidation.

We Democrats are not blameless.

Most refused to vote for any cuts, relying on Republicans and a few fiscally responsible Democrats like me to provide narrow majorities for necessary budget cuts. Some Democrats argued that we should restore cuts by using any remaining stimulus dollars and raising taxes.

That is not a good idea.

Raiding the stimulus would subtract $200 million from next year's balance sheet. It would also raise spending in 2010 by $200 million, requiring $200 million more just to sustain the increase in 2011. **The net result would add $400 million to the 2011 deficit.** Instead of stability, blowing the stimulus would guarantee double the cut necessary next year.

Someone has to say no. I am that someone.

These times require fiscal discipline. Democrats should move the party in this direction. It will anger special interests now, but the electorate will eventually reward leaders who restore fiscal order.

Would you rather have someone who says lunch is free?

If you do, I am not your man

Because I am telling you we can't afford steak, it's going to be peanut butter and jelly, and you have to help do the dishes afterward. It saddens me to hear politicians tell people we can afford to restore the Promise Scholarship.

It's good politics, because there are 100,000 students who lost the scholarship, and they have 200,000 parents. They like people who say we should fund the scholarships and grow angry with people like me who say we can't afford them.

The truth hurts.

The Scholarship costs $140 million. Some suggest we could pay for them by reducing a tax credit for the working poor. That is terribly wrong on two points.

First, we may *have* to cut the credit for the poor. But can Democrats really support stripping tax refunds from the working poor (individuals making less than $14,000 a year) and giving that money to college students who exceed the income limits for financial aid? Is it fair to fund scholarships with money taken from workers earning less than $14,000 a year?

I know Democrats are accused of wanting to redistribute wealth, but I didn't know that included transferring cash from the working poor to the middle class.

But there is a bigger issue.

If we have a spare $140 million, we had better put it toward next year's deficit. How could any responsible person restore cuts when we have a big deficit awaiting legislative action in February?

It's time we face reality in Michigan. Our spending habits far exceed our income. We need to take aggressive action to reach a balance.

Should we raise revenue?

According to Treasury projections, even if we freeze spending at current (post-cut) levels, we will face a deficit of $1.3 billion dollars in 2011. That is a huge sum.

But consider what it would take to restore spending cuts and then freeze spending in 2011. Using the Governor's most recent spending proposal, the deficit would rise to $2 billion. *Raising taxes that much would require an increase equal to the tax hike of 2007, plus 50% more.*

In 2007 we raised the income tax from 3.9% to 4.35%, and added a 22% surcharge to the Business Tax. We would have to do the equivalent of that, **plus 50% more**, to restore and sustain funding.

I voted for the 2007 tax increase, so I've earned some credibility here. I am no anti-tax zealot. So when I say we can't raise taxes that much and have to cut, it is coming from someone who has supported, and continues to support, taxes when they are appropriate. But a tax increase of this magnitude is unrealistic and wrong.

The Governor, House, and Senate rejected a general tax increase this year because of the poor economy. So how can anyone honestly promise citizens a restoration of cuts?

I think people deserve the truth, *especially* when it is unpleasant. Michigan is being challenged like never before. We have been blessed as one of the richest states, but we are now one of the poorest. We can accept this fate, or resist. To create a different fortune, we must change.

We have to adjust to global competition. We can deny the challenge, and try to continue the status quo. We can complain that the competition is unfair, and try to change the rules. Or we can change our approach. When challenged, we can work smarter and harder and win the competition. We have to take our cuts when necessary, and that goes for everyone, especially the leaders. It goes for government, including legislators.

Are we up to the challenge?

If we are worthy of being the children of the greatest generation, we should remember what their childhood was like. They did not live in luxury, or embrace a culture of entitlement.

Michigan's rebirth lies in rediscovering those values.

Thanks for Playing the Game
And What Do We Have For Our Losing Contestant?

I ran for the US Congress last Tuesday and was defeated by incumbent Sander Levin. I worked hard on the campaign, but in the end it wasn't close. I was beaten 3 to 1.

My friends and supporters worked hard to help me, contributed to me, and, even prayed for me. I know many of them feel bad for me and hope that I am ok.

I thank you all for your support, and I am profoundly moved by your concern. Believe me when I tell you I am fine with the result.

To quote St. Paul the Apostle: *"I have run the race. I have kept the faith."* I feel fortunate. I got to run the race I wanted to run, the way I wanted to run it. I have no regrets.

I had a great experience campaigning. I learned so much and made so many friends that I count it as a positive. Sure, it would have been nice to win. But forget Lombardi. Winning isn't everything. In fact it's vastly overrated. I certainly don't feel like a loser. I had a blast. Even knowing the result, I would do it again.

I got to run for Congress. I got to stand up for something I believe in and give people a choice. Something about that is deeply satisfying. Going into the race, I figured people had been voting for Levin and Switalski for 20 years. I wanted to know what they would do if given a choice between the two.

I got my answer. They chose Levin. And I accept that.

I will take many great things away from this campaign with me. I got up at 5 am almost every day for 2 years, and went out door to door with my friends sticking my *Insider* newsletter in people's doors. I got in good shape and lost about 15 pounds. As I regain the weight, I want to redistribute it to the right places. My belly is not a preferred destination.

I got to see magical places I'd never seen before, like the architecture on St. Louis Street in Ferndale, the Star Bakery in Oak Park, the stately mansions of Pleasant Ridge and the charms of "Peasant Ridge." I had a ball knocking doors in the 'hood in Southfield and Oak Park, and was warmly embraced by many denizens of Hazel Park.

Most valuable were the friendships I gained. How can I be a loser when I gained the support of people like Steve and Sharon

Gallop? Steve worked for Dave Bonior for 30 years and is a thoughtful, creative, and fascinating person with encyclopedic knowledge of an eclectic variety of subjects. He is an accomplished chef, connoisseur of beer and ethnic food, and has an infectious zest for life that I find irresistible. He was there every weekday at 5:15 am for a 5:30 lit drop.

I met Andi Kola, who was an indifferent student in High School, before beginning to apply himself at MCCC and is now an A student at U of M. Andi came to America from Albania at age 10. He dropped every day with me the summer of 2009.

When I wanted to show my son Liam what college was like, Andi arranged for us to attend 2 of his classes in Ann Arbor. Andi blew one of his classmates out of the water during class discussion, and Liam was high-fiving him after class. It was a fantastic experience for Liam and got him fired up for University.

None of this would have happened if I hadn't run.

I'd known Debbie Sieradzki since I coached her son Chris in soccer as a boy. But I got to know her for real when we began dropping every weekend, meeting me as far away as Southfield for a 4-hour drop. Debbie is a high-priced health care consultant. I can't even believe how much she helped me, plus she is fast.

I will never forget dropping Roseville with my cousin Jon in the dark, in knee-deep snow during a blizzard, or how blessed I am to have met Suzanne Gauvreau, an opera singer, cancer survivor, and an organizer of the Arlington Street Block Party, which I got to invite Bill Clinton to (he didn't show).

I got fantastic help from Greg Nasto, whose sister I hung out with in High School. Greg created a website for me that was so far superior to anything else out in the blogosphere that he should be knighted. His work, along with his assistant Vince Cracchiolo, was the most fun and creative part of the campaign, and he did it all with virtually no budget.

My ace intern, the incomparable Ashley Morris, dumbfounded me with her talents, and Marie Gordon, my staff attorney, went home and hand-made me lit drop bags. Jeff Minore brought his whole family from Grand Rapids to help campaign.

Zvonko Blazevski organized the Macedonian Partisans for me on weekends, and I had to laugh when Chuck Woolaver, whose wife Katy is my 2nd grade flame, got so excited when I made him a multi-precinct captain. He organized "C" Company to do the massive Rivergate subdivision and more. Janine Brown, Anthony Bartalone and Jodi Debrecht were tireless helpers in many ways, and I can never thank them enough. Golfing buddy John Zuccarini was incredibly generous, and my Sacred Heart pals, Dave Komosinski, Nancy Kreutz, Shelly and Ben Ratkov, the Billy Mott Clan, Frank Redmond and Dave Brown and Carmella Juliano all helped me knock out Ferndale in a single day.

Maria Bartalone broke her foot dropping with me one morning. She also fell down one winter day before delivering a single piece of literature, a record that will never be surpassed. She and beautiful young attorneys Janelle Smith and Lisa Ryan guaranteed a spike in male volunteers as long as they were in the field.

Mike O'Meara organized the Irish, which many said couldn't be done. When his red-headed girlfriend Lauren showed up in a smart skirt for a lit drop, I knew we had a chance with the toffs. I ordered new uniforms for everyone, but sadly none complied.

Eastpointe Councilwoman Veronica Klinefelt has always been there for me, even after I lost and needed help picking up signs. If you've ever driven in steel poles with a bonger, you'll know how hard trustee Dean Reynolds worked putting up 100 big signs in Clinton Township. Rich Steenland pulled off a similar job in Roseville. Danny Petkoff and my sign crew completed enormous tasks in what seemed a few hours.

Sam and Beth Aiuto have been a godsend over the years, but they took it to a new level by bringing me into the 21st century with my email, website, facebook and databases. My son Liam and Sherman Abdo kept my Facebook current and dispelled my moniker of "Jimmy Naypals."

Tony Caputo came to my rescue after I put Roma's wedding ring in hock at *Ron's Pawn Shop*. He got his friends to raise a ton of money for me, and kept me afloat at the end. Tony and his assistant Pam Kroll are decisive, efficient, and consummate professionals, which my rag-tag approach to elections could use more of. Lou and Lisa Corey were exceedingly generous, but they were even more fun to hang out with.

Theresa and Joe Vitale worked their extended family, putting out signs, stuffing envelopes, and organizing the entire GOTV effort. They were irreplaceable. Rita and Morris Wilson, Dee Calder, Jenny and Denise DiGiovanni stuffed envelopes like there was no tomorrow. Johnny Boedeker and Mark Ward helped me in many ways, and Mark's family even got his 6-year old to make GOTV calls for me. Steve Ratkov rescued me from a long prison term by correcting numerous errors in my campaign finance reports. Roseanne and Irene Kepler embarrass me with their support and friendship, as did my RHS pals, valedictorian Lavern Orlang, who I hadn't seen in 30 years before we had a beer at Club 11, Kathy Jakubiac, Kathy Scott, Jeff Brantley, and the tireless Donna Taylor, the ringleader of the whole effort.

My family put up with me and this campaign for 2 years and never complained. My wife Roma is a saint, plus she lost 60 pounds on Weightwatchers.

How lucky can I get?

My son Liam and nephew Sebastian are superior campaigners. I brought in my nephews, Andrew from Baltimore and Christopher from Glasgow, Scotland, to help out. My 84-year old mother Nancy worked especially hard when *The Insider* contained stories about her. As usual, my sister in law Helena Heaney outperformed everyone.

I had a series of adventures with *Inventor Extraordinaire* John Van Camp, who was the brains behind the most unique big sign placements ever. We did the signs atop the old *Macomb Daily* building, on the wind-swept hills of the Marsac Gravel Pit, and on the roof of Roseville landmark *Club 11*. Each one was an unforgettable experience I will always treasure.

I really don't deserve friends like these. But somehow I have them. I have no money to speak of, but I consider myself richer than any billionaire, because you couldn't buy friends like these.

I lost an election, but so what?

My life is all the richer for having had this experience. Thank you all for the honor of serving you in government. I have had a great run for 21 years, and I will always treasure those years. I hope I served you well, and I look forward to new challenges in the years ahead.

Youth Will be Served

Requiem for the Double Date

Where do we draw the line between freedom and safety?

It's not an easy task when balancing such mundane concerns as carpooling, double-dating, and young drivers.

House Bill 4600 would have restricted first year drivers, 16 years of age, to one unrelated passenger in the car with them.

The bill was a response to a terrible accident in Livingston County, when a van full of youngsters veered off the road, hit a tree, and resulted in the death of 6 youths. HB 4600 was introduced in the House to limit the number of passengers accompanying first year drivers, thereby reducing distractions, and hopefully saving lives.

The bill faced a contentious road in the House, where it was nearly defeated before achieving a narrow passage after significant amendments were added. The most significant change specified that drivers could be exempt from the law if they had a note in the glovebox from a parent saying extra passengers were ok.

Legislators struggled with the issue, weighing improved safety on one hand versus state intrusion, parental control, and individual freedom on the other.

I had grave misgivings about the bill when it came to the Senate. I understood the position of the advocates for the bill, who thought HB 4600 would save people's lives.

But I took a constitutional oath about matters of individual rights and freedoms, and I take it very seriously. Especially when it comes to young people. They are a convenient target for aggressive laws seeking to control and manage behavior. Careful readers of *The Insider* may recall that I fought hard against an earlier bill providing jail time for minors in possession of alcohol, but was defeated (*Insider* Vol 8, no 5, *Turning Our Kids into Criminals*).

I geared up for another battle.

While well-intentioned, the bill went too far. Michigan has been a leader in driver safety for new drivers. For several years now we have had a graduated driver's license program which puts restrictions on new drivers, allowing them to drive only with a parent, then later only certain hours of the day, until they get full unrestricted privileges, at age 17, if they have a clean record. The new system has been very successful in reducing accidents among young drivers.

So we have already addressed this issue.

HB 4600 was imprecise and might suffer the law of unintended consequences. One of my colleagues pointed out that passage of this bill would have meant even more young drivers on the road, since they couldn't share rides, and thus probably more accidents.

Clearly, HB 4600 was important. It would affect every kid and family in the state. It would punish the good with the bad. The Declaration of Independence says that the pursuit of happiness is one of our God-given, inalienable rights. We are supposed to protect those rights.

Yet this bill would have banned kids from carpooling to school, or borrowing dad's car to go to a game, a concert, or out for a hamburger with their friends. It would have significantly constrained their pursuit of happiness. Don't you remember the exhilarating thrill of freedom you felt when you first hit the road with your pals?

Isn't there some value to that?

The bill would have kept kids from giving a stranded friend a ride home from a party or basketball game. Any decent kid would have offered the ride anyway. Then we would have turned Good Samaritans into lawbreakers.

We don't take this approach with gun rights, and we are correct not to.

We don't take everyone's guns away because of the unlawful actions of a few criminals. Why would we restrict this right, which is far more widely exercised and cherished?

I argued these points during a speech on the Senate floor, and saved my best argument for last.

"Mr. President," I concluded. "I remember a steamy August night in the back seat of a car with Patty Otto on a double date."

A knowing ripple of nostalgia swept the Senate.

"This bill would outlaw the double date. I refuse to believe the Senate could be that callous and cruel."

HB 4600 was one of those unpredictable issues where you never knew what would happen. Most bills do not come to the floor unless the leadership believes there are sufficient votes for passage. But this one was very close. Both support and opposition cut across party lines. The Senate often passes appropriation bills unanimously, expending millions of dollars with minimal discussion.

But this debate raged for over an hour.

In comparison with billion dollar budget bills, this issue might seem insignificant. But I think it was important, because it affected everyone in the state and it involved freedom. And freedom is priceless.

HB 4600 was defeated 17-21.

I called up Patty Otto's mother, Mary Lou, and told her that her daughter had helped defeat some bad legislation. She was so proud of her daughter.

I sent Patty, who now lives in Washington State, a copy of my speech in the Senate Journal, and reiterated to her that her considerable talents had resulted in good public policy for Michigan.

"Everyone here really wants to meet you," I told her. "Especially the men. Is it OK if I give out your phone number?"

Looking back, it was a great day to be in Senate. It was one of those rare moments where people were unsure, and listened and thought and made up their minds on the floor over what to do. The speakers on both sides of the debate made good points and kept to the issue.

I felt lucky to be part of such an institution.

And I was humbled by the privilege of representing you on matters of such importance.

November 2004

Minors in Possession: Turning Our Kids Into Criminals

Most people know deer season opened in November, but few realize that the legislature also declared open season on Michigan Kids.

Last month the Senate passed a bill that provides jail time for *Minors in Possession of Alcohol (MIP)*. Not to be outdone, the House passed a bill, HB 4600, that limits young drivers to a single passenger in their car.

The two bills might sound good if you think we need to crack down on kids, but both lack a basic understanding of human behavior. They could also have a negative impact on thousands of Michigan families.

It's already against the law for anyone under the age of 21 to possess alcohol. In fact, the legislature just increased the penalties for MIPS four years ago. But it's legal for 19-year olds to drink in Canada. And in 2002 the *Michigan Court of Appeals* ruled in *Michigan v Rutledge* that it was OK for a minor to drink legally in Canada and come home to Michigan.

Apparently that proposition is too radical for the Michigan legislature.

I doubt many legislators read the decision before rushing to overrule the Court. I doubt they gave the issue a fraction of the thought the Appeals Court did. I suspect this is because minors don't vote in large numbers. But if adults lack the memory to recall their own actions at age 19, maybe we can summon that imagination to see what further criminalizing a diluted definition of *possession* would mean for the typical teenager.

SB 637 changes current law in two ways.

1. It redefines *possession* to include *"presence in the body."* And that presence can be as low as .02 percent of blood alcohol, which is a trace amount.

2. It provides the option of jail time for repeat offenders.

I attempted to amend the bill to restore the Appeals Court's definition of *possession*, meaning *to have on one's person or to have control of*. That's the word's common use. We all ought to beware of laws that distort the common meaning of words, especially in criminal matters. If Truth in Sentencing dictates that *Minimum means Minimum*, then Truth in Prosecution should dictate that *Possession means Possession.*

I also tried to increase .02 to .08, which means kids would probably have to have had at least two beers.

Both amendments failed.

So here's where that leaves us.

If we are saying the mere presence of trace amounts of alcohol in a minor's system is criminal possession, consider the implications. If that is possession, then minors who ingest mouthwash, cough syrup, a rum raisin ice cream cone or grandma's vanilla flavored Christmas cookies are criminals. And I suppose grandma and the ice cream man and the grocery clerk are guilty of furnishing alcohol to a minor. Maybe the Eucharistic minister who offers the common cup of wine should also be locked up.

True, current law grants an exception for generally recognized religious ceremonies. Maybe the police will reconsider when the stop a *Gratiot Avenue* cruiser after Saturday Nite Vigil Mass. Or maybe they'll just say *"Yeah. Right. Go tell it to the Judge."* A good lawyer and a few thousand dollars later, the kid might even be exonerated.

That kid might be your kid. And your few thousand.

If the presence of trace elements of illegal substances in the body constitutes criminal possession, adults may be personally affected. If we start analyzing people's hair samples, someone is just a poppy seed muffin away from a positive screen for narcotics.

Are we sure we want to water down the meaning of *possession?*

Given all these problems, just why is this bill necessary?

Are we suddenly being overwhelmed by rampant alcohol abuse by the Youth of Michigan?

No.

I doubt kids are drinking any more today than they did 20, 30, or 50 years ago in Michigan, or 1000 years ago among the Vikings.

They probably drink less.

In fact, the State Court Administrator's Office reports that MIP convictions have dropped nearly 1000 a year the last three years. The current system appears to be working. Yet we are being asked to misconstrue the meaning of *possession* and provide for jail time if our kids drink a swig of beer.

What is it that has made us so desperate?

The Michigan Court of Appeals issued a decision last year that said it was not a crime for minors to drink legally in Canada and then come home to Michigan.

I think it is wrong to try to manipulate the meaning of words, distort our laws, and put kids in jail for doing something that is patently legal and in a broader sense is more accurately characterized as juvenile misbehavior. Current law appropriately penalizes such misbehavior with fines up to $500, plus court costs.

But we want jail time.

Under SB 637, we are prepared to brand our own children as criminals, categorizing them as substance abusers, compel them to undergo therapy, put them on probation for a year, charge them thousands of dollars for these privileges, scar them with a criminal record that may limit their aspirations for the rest of their lives, and ultimately put them in jail.

All in the name of helping them. Because a kid celebrates his 19th birthday while home on leave from the War in Iraq by going to Canada with his father, and having a beer.

Kids are not stupid.

They know when they are being abused as part of somebody's *"get tough"* agenda. They have a keen eye for injustice and hypocrisy. Does a college sophomore at a campus kegger really need a year of counseling and monthly visits to his probation officer? Do kids in the basement at a New Year's Eve Party need to perform 100 hours of community service, extensive rehab, and undergo substance abuse screening? Will this make them respect the law, obey their elders, and believe in the values of our society?

No. It will do exactly the opposite.

Have we lost all perspective?

Underage drinking is a problem. Good policy would manage this problem within acceptable limits. This draconian law based on zero tolerance sets decent kids up to become criminals.

The jails in Macomb County are full. When we hit 7 straight days over capacity, the Chief Judge has to let somebody out. We just let 49 prisoners out this month. That was after letting out 100 early in November. The judges will have to let more out if we have to make room for kids who have trace amounts of alcohol in their systems.

Is this how we want our kids treated and our jails run?

December 2003

Rock the High School Dropouts

The Archangel Gabriel, moonlighting as a High School Counselor, had one last appointment for the day. Jeff Spicoli had just turned 16, flunked Algebra, and wanted to quit school.

"What do you like, Jeff?" Gabriel asked. "Music? Art? I can get you in band or choir. How about a tech class? Electronics? Cooking? Do you like cars?"

Spicoli started thinking, and his brain needed the exercise. Gabriel had a chance to save him, but this year the Michigan Legislature had made the job a lot tougher. Michigan enacted new standards requiring Algebra, plus 3 more *even harder* math courses. Even for Gabriel, that's a tough sell, and the dropout rate was rising.

Gabriel knew he was at risk of losing Spicoli to his arch rival.

After 5 o'clock, Gabriel went to the Good Lord for a bailout.

"Lucifer's been in the market for years," Gabriel cried. "He's been buying and selling souls for centuries. We're fighting with 2 hands tied behind our backs. We can't compete."

"What are you asking for?" shot back *St. Michael the Archangel*, as the Lord sat listening. Michael is God's *Chief of Staff for Administrative Affairs*, and *General Hatchet Man*.

"I want to deal in commodities," begged Gabriel. "I want authority to extend the lives of people who are doing the Lord's work. Lucifer's offering the bad ones *riches, power, and pleasures*. I just want to level the playing field."

The Lord nodded his assent, and Michael laid out the parameters. "On a pilot basis, we will grant you one extension. Make it a good one," he warned sternly. And as he sharpened the famous ax he used to drive Lucifer from Heaven, he took a parting shot at Gabriel.

"And don't do anything to embarrass us."

In a snap Gabriel was gone and materialized at the *Immaculate Heart of Mary Motherhouse* for aged nuns in Monroe, Michigan. He'd already chosen his candidate. He met the Grim Reaper at the door, just in the Nick of time.

"Not today," he told the Reaper breezily. "Special Dispensation from the Big Guy." He handed the Grim One an *Emergency Stay of Execution* with St. Michael's seal, and the Reaper sheathed his sickle and trudged silently away. "Behold, Sister," announced Gabriel as he entered Sister Mary Rock's room. Rock was clutching her rosary in bed with 3 blankets over her.

"You again," sighed Rock. "I was expecting the Reaper."

"I spent him packing," said Gabriel. "I've got an offer you can't refuse."

"I'm all ears," said Rock. Gabriel caught himself before poking fun at Rock's especially large nose, her most prominent feature. She was a shade over 4 feet tall, and seemed ageless despite her 112 years. She'd spent 74 years teaching, and put the *Fear of God* into wee Catholic schoolchildren. After forced retirement at age 92, she'd spent the last 20 years at the Motherhouse, growing increasingly frail.

"We need you," Gabriel pled.

"Michigan's got themselves into an H E double-hockey stick of a mess. Their economy is in shambles, people are out of work and losing their houses."

"I'm a teacher, not an economist," objected Rock.

"Thank God for that," quipped Gabriel, crossing himself. "That's where you come in. To fix this problem long term, we have to teach kids not to make the same financial mistakes their parents made. And besides that, the state has toughened up the High School Curriculum, added more mathematics, and kids are flunking and dropping out like flies."

Rock's eyes narrowed. "I'd like to help," she whispered, "but my flesh is weak."

"I've negotiated an extra year for you," Gabriel pitched. "Plus you'll be in your prime – just like you felt at age 70. All we need is for you to set up our new Math Class. It's called **Financial Literacy.** That apostate Senator Switalski finally passed a worthwhile bill. The kids are gonna love it."

"Things must have changed in 20 years," moaned Rock. "The last kids I had hated math."

"Damned Lucifer's got them all loving money. But we'll use that to get them interested in math. We'll kill two birds with one stone. Even if they flunked Algebra, when they pass *Financial Literacy* their math confidence will soar. After that, they _will_ pass Algebra. I've got it all figured out. You'll have these kids eating numbers out of your hand," promised Gabriel.

Rock signed the papers after reluctantly agreeing to Gabriel's insistence that she not wear her *Habit*, the old nun's uniform, during class hours. She started teaching at South Central High School the following week.

"Class," Sister Rock began insistently, just audible above the din.

"Class."

"CLASS!!!"

For a moment there was silence, then Spicoli, the class buffoon, chimed in.

"Lighten up, sister."

Sr. Mary Rock drew herself up to the full 4 feet of her frame, placing her nose within a centimeter of Spicoli's proboscis. Her piercing eyes looked straight into his disheveled soul.

"I don't like what I see," she state flatly.

An uneasy silence ensued.

"This course in Financial Literacy will count towards one of the four math classes you are required to pass for Graduation," began Rock.

"Let's begin with a story problem. Close your eyes. You have just won the Michigan State Lottery for $10 million. Do you take the money in a lump sum up front, or do you collect it in equal payments over 20 years?"

Spicoli's hand shot up.

"Up front," he suggested. "That way I can hire Nickelback to play my 18th Birthday Party."

"OK," replied Rock. "You understand, Mr. Spicoli, that because of the time value of money, your payout will be discounted to only $5 million if you take if up front?" asked Rock.

"Wha-wha-wha-What?" stammered Spicoli.

"And you will have to pay state, federal and local taxes on the $5 million. Let's get to work. Any volunteers to go to the board and do 4.35% state income tax on $5 Million? How about Federal Income tax? It's not a flat rate, like Michigan has. It's progressive. The rate goes up the higher your compensation," explained Rock.

"That sounds Socialist," said J.T. Plummer from his desk in the back of the room. "I just won't pay."

"Sister, what if I take it over 20 years?" asked Spicoli.

"You get the full $10 million, in annual payments of $500,000. Who can tell me how much that is monthly, weekly, and hourly?" continued Rock.

The class broke into their Cooperative Learning Groups to do various calculations, and then share, critique, and debate their answers and determine the most fiscally responsible choices.

"That $500,000 is less than $10,000 a week," explained Spicoli, gnawing at his pencil.

"What do you take home after taxes?" reminded Rock.

I still have to subtract that," said Spicoli ruefully. "I'd better settle for the *Tribtones* at my birthday party."

"OK, class," said Rock. "Tomorrow we will be going to the casino, which is my desk, to analyze the probabilities in Blackjack, Roulette, Slots, Craps, and Texas Hold 'em. Then you can determine which game best favors the House or the player, and when it is best to not play."

It was standing room only when they studied mortgages with adjustable rates and foreclosures and interest only loans and balloon payments. As a bonus they did the numbers on various student loans. Parent-teacher night set a record for attendance that week.

By the end of the semester, kids started bringing homework to school. They brought credit card bills, contracts to buy or lease cars, and pension options at the request of their parents to see if they were being fiscally wise or foolish. Kids started building household budgets and balancing checkbooks. After a few years, personal debt shrank, and the housing crisis subsided.

Gabriel entered his office one morning to find St. Mary Rock waiting for him.

"I think I can get you another year's extension," Gabriel offered cheerily.

Rock cut him off with an upraised palm.

"I want 5 years. And no more class time," she ordered. "Spicoli and I are getting married and moving out West. We're creating a startup to do these classes online. Open to all ages."

Gabriel stood motionless.

"Got it? And you can keep this," she added. She tossed Gabriel a brown paper grocery bag and left.

Inside was her navy blue and black Habit, and on the bottom were a pair of standard issue nun's platform shoes with thick soles and 6 inch chunky heels. Turns out Rock was only 3 ½ feet tall!

Gabriel leaned back in his chair. His initiative had been an overwhelming success.

St. Michael might blow a fuse, but he was sure the *Big Guy* would back him.

December 2008

Governing the Cherokee Nation

As part of my job, I get to visit a lot of schools. I have toured the Michigan Virtual High School and addressed the annual Education Conference in the Upper Peninsula. I have been in hundreds of classrooms. I have lectured on politics to University post graduates, and read nursery rhymes to kindergartners with my coat turned inside out and a Scottish Tartan Wig on my head.

But every time I think I have seen and done it all, I discover something truly inspiring.

I received a call recently asking me to come visit Ruth Cummins' 5th grade class at Cherokee Elementary, which is in the Rivergate Subdivision in Clinton Township. The students had visited Lansing and had some questions about how the Legislature works. I routinely make such visits. Often I divide the class into a legislature, make all the girls senators and all the boys representatives, have them elect a governor, and then try to pass a law. Sometimes I have them vote on whether to start school earlier, stay later, and have Fridays off. Sometimes I have them choose whether Chicken McNuggets, pizza, or cheeseburgers should be the official fast food of the state of Michigan. I usually decide how elaborate to get once I see how energetic the kids are.

But I was not prepared for what I found.

The students had elected an executive Branch, including a President and a Treasurer, but most of the students were either members of the Senate or the House. This was determined by drawing names out of a hat. They had a Senate Leader and a Speaker of the House. The Judiciary rounded out the three branches of government. Ms. Cummins, the teacher, doubled as the Supreme Court. Her sole power was to rule on the constitutionality of any legislation passed.

When the Cherokee Government was established in the first semester, the Legislature quickly passed a bill granting an extended holiday from school. The President eagerly signed the bill, but the new law was immediately overturned by Chief Justice Cummins. The law violated the Constitution, which consisted of the compiled rules and policies of the school.

Drat! Foiled again.

As the students answered my questions, I was slowly realizing how elaborate, and how realistic, the adventures of the Cherokee Government were. Their project approximated an actual Legislature. The parallels were spooky. The students felt they were doing something wrong, because they had only been able to pass 13 bills the whole year. I reassured them that although there were thousands of bills introduced each session of the legislature, only a couple of hundred actually make it into law. It is intentionally hard to pass a law, which is how the founders designed the system. That creates stability in the law. And the Cherokee experience exactly reflected that reality.

They were unhappy about how much they fought over legislation and how hard it was to reach agreement. They were embarrassed that sometimes people got into terrible arguments and got very mad at each other. I told them about the times people were so angry that they cried during speeches on the floor. This made them feel a lot better, because again it meant their government was realistic.

After the Court struck down their first effort, the Legislature turned to the top priority for any government body. How will we get paid? This was probably the most realistic part of the entire exercise. They decided that students would earn money for things like completing all their assignments or doing extra credit work.

This is where the class project entered a new level of sophistication. They created their own money and their own economy. The $20 bill had Treasurer Nick Kutskill's face on it. There was a class store, where students could buy trinkets or used books, the right to a comfortable seat during story time, or even the teacher's seat. They could even buy insurance to render their own seat untouchable.

As the students revealed each new level of complexity to this entire scheme, I grew giddy. The kids were eager to tell me about their experiences, and wanted me to take sides in their disputes over legislation they couldn't pass. The Senate leader had wanted to establish Security Guards at the class store because the Treasurer was unhappy about disorderly transactions and the dangers of financial chicanery.

But the House would have none of it. It is the People's Chamber, after all.

I suggested to them, that sometimes, if the other chamber won't pass a bill you really want, you can hold up one of their bills until they agree to compromise. They were fascinated by the concept of horse-trading, and couldn't wait to try their hands at wheeling and dealing.

I felt a little bad about telling them about some of these cynical legislative tricks. But having experienced gridlock firsthand, these kids recognized the necessity of such tactics to move an agenda. I doubt that most college political science students have as sound a grasp of the intricacies of the legislative process that these 5th graders had acquired.

At this point the students revealed the greatest innovation of all. At the start of the second semester, Ms. Cummins had introduced the concept of taxes. Students were given a tax bill, and a huge battle ensued over whether to have a graduated tax system or a flat tax. Students who had worked hard and accumulated a lot of money were outraged by the concept of a graduated tax, where you pay a higher percentage the more money you have. Those without much money had no problem raising the take from the higher income brackets. There were passionate debates over the structure of the tax system.

What could be more lifelike? And as a result of this debate and how invested in the topic they were, the kids learned a great deal. These students knew more about progressive and regressive and flat taxes than most of the electorate. I came away truly impressed.

I am working now to find a way to spread the Cherokee Government to other schools. This is surely the best way to teach government and social studies I have ever seen.

Hats off to Ruth Cummins and her Cherokee Government. Now if only we can get the Legislature to act like those kids.

July 2006

Single-Gender Schools

The Michigan Senate, by a 33-5 vote, passed legislation on June 15 that would allow school districts to establish single-gendered schools and classrooms. Senate Bill 1296 will head to the House, where another version is being worked on.

When I was in junior high school, about 90 percent of my attention and energy was focused on a tall, blonde-haired girl named Karla. I can assure you that is a conservative estimate. If I had been able to redirect that youthful energy on my studies, who knows what I might have accomplished. I don't know that I would have cured cancer or written the great American novel or perfected the fuel cell, but I surely would be further along toward achieving my ultimate goal of world domination.

Once in awhile, we need to be brave, to be bold, and to think outside of the box, although I find myself in disagreement with many of my friends on this bill. I have pushed for this legislation for six years, ever since I was a member of the Michigan House. I have received much flak for the idea but I toughed it out and kept pushing for it. Single-gender education deserves a chance. This bill is about choice. No one is forced to create a single-gender school or classroom, but the protection of state law is there for those schools that so choose.

Why would someone choose to create single-gender education? Clearly, for some students, parents, and educators it is a valuable option. Research shows that junior high school math and science participation and performance by girls begins to fall significantly in junior high and that single-gender classes can reverse that decline and help many women realize their full God-given potential.

I oppose discrimination as strongly as anyone, and I believe that this bill is not discriminatory, but instead is a positive act to empower both boys and girls. I welcome the debate about the constitutionality of this bill. I submit that equal treatment does not have to be the exact same treatment. Men and women are different and policy should be designed to allow each to flourish.

Title IX has allowed women's athletics to flourish, not by making women play football, but by spending equivalent scholarship dollars on other sports such as woman's soccer. That's why the U.S. women won the World Cup in 1999. Now if only the men's team can keep up the pace, we would be a true soccer power. Keeping everything the same for everyone ignores our differences. We should celebrate our diversity by tailoring education to help everyone achieve their potential in unique ways.

Birmingham has single-gender classes. They are hugely popular with a waiting list of 100 for 28 slots. You have to win the lottery to get into that class. Malcolm X Academy in Detroit posted the highest math scores among the city's 77 middle schools and was second in the state among 780 schools. Detroit wants to open two single-gender schools. We are all concerned about educational excellence in the city. This approach offers an opportunity to achieve significant gains, and it could act as a trailblazer for others considering this approach.

The South Lake Public School District in St. Clair Shores has declared that it plans to test out its own program at the middle school level. According to the Detroit News, the district has 27 girls and 23 boys that voluntarily enrolled in single-gendered math and language arts classes. Science, social studies and other classes would still be conducted in the traditional manner. So there is demand out there to try something new in the schools.

June 2006

Confessions of a Professional Student

My father always stressed to me the importance of getting a good education. He incessantly preached the importance of education to me and my six brothers and sisters. We listened, but as children sometimes do, we listened too well.

My parents valued education enough to pay to send us to Catholic School, but after my sophomore year in high school at Sacred Heart in Roseville, the school closed. I did my last two years at Roseville High, met an entirely new group of people, and made a lot of new friends. I hated that my school closed, but I felt lucky that I got to see two different systems, the public and private schools. I saw how they were different, and that there wasn't just one way to do things in life. I also had to learn how to get along with very different kinds of people. Nowadays, this is called diversity. For me, it was a very good experience because it opened a new world to me.

When I finished high school, I wanted to go away to college. My parents, with 7 kids, didn't have enough money to send me to college, but my Dad gave me a job making tombstones in his shop in Detroit, the Sheldon Granite Company.

I saved my money and went away to Louisiana State University in Baton Rouge. My older brother Mark had gone there for a couple of years, when Pistol Pete Maravich was scoring 44 a game, so I knew a few people through him, and tuition was dirt cheap. Even with out-of-state tuition, it was cheaper than Michigan. Plus, Louisiana is a great state. It is part of a distinctive part of the country, the Old South, and yet it is unique, with New Orleans, the jazz and Cajuns and Creoles and the French influence. And it was warm down there. So I figured it would be a great adventure.

LSU became something of a family tradition among the Switalskis. My younger sister Monica ended up going there after I left, and now my 12-year old son, Liam, has informed me that he intends to go there.

I felt an urge to go somewhere completely new and alien, where no one knew me, and completely remake myself. Having a big nurturing family is great, but it can be confining, and I wanted to be liberated from all my past influences and go off in a new direction. I was determined to go there and study hard.

Baton Rouge lived up to my high expectations. I lived in the football stadium, where the irrepressible Kingfish, Huey P. Long, had built dormitories under the seats. I was poor and lived on one Big Mac a day when the cafeteria was closed. I pedaled a raggedy bicycle to the Mississippi levee and read there in the afternoon sun. I worked in the Plantation Room restaurant of the student union, and learned to love gumbo and red beans and rice and corn muffins. I saved my pennies, walked to the bookstore and bought a philosophy book like Descartes or Plato or Burke and spend the day in bed reading it, until the stadium throbbed in anticipation of Tiger football that evening.

After a year of hard work, I won a President's scholarship from the University, which simply gave me in-state tuition. But that was huge, because tuition was only $167 a semester, no matter how many hours you took. Ever mindful of a bargain, I would load up with the max of 19 or 20 hours, and I got into the honors program, which was the best educational experience I ever had. The Honors Program was team taught by top faculty and had about 50 students, with 3 hours of lecture and 3 hours of seminars, reading the Great Books of Western Civilization.

I switched my major from History to something really arcane, Classical Languages, the study of ancient Latin and Greek. I got my Bachelors degree in that, and won a full scholarship to Duke University's Ph.D program in Classics.

After a year at Duke, I made an important decision. Job prospects were not good for Classics graduates. The Ph.D grads ahead of me were waiting on tables. And during my last two years at LSU, I had become increasingly interested, even obsessed, with politics. I was working hard at a career with slim opportunities, in a field that was the epitome of the ivory tower. I felt like I wanted to mix it up in this world, the rough and tumble of current affairs, and not lock myself away to contemplate the eternal verities.

I walked away from Duke and my scholarship after one year and turned up at LSU the next fall. I applied to the History Graduate School, interviewed with the Department Chair and won an assistantship on the spot. It was just enough to live on and pay my tuition, and I found a great place on Park Boulevard with two Louisiana buddies. I also got a chance to work offshore on an oil rig, an incredible experience, and got a job as a stringer covering high school basketball for the St. Tammany Farmer. These were some of the most enjoyable years of my life.

I met my future wife, Roma, during this time. She was a foreign student from Glasgow, Scotland, working in the Louisiana State Archives for the summer while doing research for her Ph.D in History from the University of Pennsylvania, where she was on full scholarship.

My father monitored my progress with discomfort. I was getting an education, but maybe a little bit too much education. He would frequently ask my brother Mark, who was in law school, "When are you going to be done with school and start putting some money in the kitty?" Mark, who is a judge now, would patiently say how much was left of his 3 years in law school. It wouldn't be long before my dad would ask him the same question again. All us kids would just laugh.

With me, my dad would say, "Mickey, you've got to get a program." His point was that there had to be a purpose to an education. It shouldn't be an end in itself, especially if that meant not contributing to the kitty.

But I went on my merry way.

I was 26 when I finished my Masters in History from LSU, and it was time to make a decision. I had a job offer at the St. Tammany Farmer, as editor of the one-person newspaper. Louisiana would be a great place to live. Life was slower down there, and as a Yankee, I seemed to move at a faster pace than the locals. So just by being normal I figured I could get ahead. I'd secretly wanted to be a farmer since raising chickens as a kid, and maybe this was my chance.

But at Roma's urging, I applied to a graduate program in Politics at the University of Aberdeen in Scotland. I was very interested in Foreign Policy and it was one of five programs in the world recommended in a newsletter I subscribed to. She was heading back to Scotland and it seemed like fate might play a hand in our lives.

Imagine my delight when I won a full scholarship to Aberdeen and fulfilled a boyhood dream of going to school in Europe. I was accepted into the Masters of Letters program in Politics, and the stipend gave me free tuition and enough money to live on for the yearlong program. Goodbye, St. Tammany Parish and hello, Scotland!

I flew from New Orleans to Atlanta to London, and took the train 8 hours to Glasgow, where Roma lived. I still remember coming through the clouds to see the bright patchwork of fields and hedgerows and stone dykes of Britain, and struggling through a misty Victoria Station carrying a backpack, two big suitcases and a typewriter.

My educational experience was most profound in Aberdeen. I booked it in Louisiana, and I enjoyed the culture. But nothing beats immersion in a foreign country for opening your eyes to the world around you, making you appreciate what we have in this country, and making you question basic assumptions about the way things are or have to be.

The courses were great, the medieval setting was beautiful, and the people and their speech were fascinating and the creature comforts were backwards. This was more than education of the mind. It was a new experience for the whole body.

Halfway through the year, just as I began a planned excursion into the British countryside with Roma, I got a call. My father had died suddenly of a heart attack. I returned home the next day on the longest flight of my life, silently weeping most of the journey.

There was some discussion of my remaining, but I wanted to finish and I returned for the Spring Term. But a chapter was closing in my life. Death has a way of refocusing your attention on the relentless passage of time and makes you assess your place in the world. I was 27 now. My friends were married, with kids and making their careers.

I made the most of my time. I studied hard, but I also took up golf on the ancient Kings Links across from the College, where golf has been played for 500 years. I drank lots of Guinness. I passed my exams and my professor hired me to do research on a study of prospects for defense specialization within NATO. I did that instead of working on my dissertation, and then spent the money I earned on a trip to Italy with Roma.

I returned home, at the height of the 1982 recession, the worst economic time in Michigan I have ever seen. There were no jobs to be had. I eventually cobbled together 5 different part-time jobs, all at the same time, to manage a semi-living wage. I saved my pennies living at home with my mother and little brother Matt.

I worked half-heartedly on my dissertation, but never finished it. My Scottish Professor, a great thinker and excellent writer named David Greenwood, called with an offer of an assistantship at Cornell in Ithaca, New York. A prof from LSU called offering a job on a congressional campaign.

But I rejected both. I was determined to build my part-time jobs into a real job here near my family. My life as an itinerant student was over. Like many people, in the years ahead I took the odd course at Wayne State and U of M Dearborn, to help me with my real job. But my long and pleasant run as a professional student was over.

Within 3 years, I was gainfully employed by General Dynamics and married Roma, luring her away from her beloved Scotland. We've been married 21 years now.

Now that has been a real education.

March 2006

Sports

Play Ball

The Winter is Past,
The Rain is over and gone;
The Flowers appear on the Earth;
The time of the Song of Birds has come,
And the Voice of the Turtle is heard in our Land.

Yes, baseball season is underway. And my son Liam, who is in 7th grade, loves sports. For countless weeks, I had been urging him to play for his school team, the *St. Angela Cougars*. Liam had a banner season in basketball, his first love, and has been playing great soccer.

But baseball was another matter.

I couldn't convince my son that he should play baseball, despite arguments that I thought were compelling:

1. The Cougars have really cool uniforms.
2. He would be playing with his friends and get to hang out with 8th graders.
3. It might be the only time in his life that he gets to play organized baseball.
4. He might be really good at it.
5. It would make him a better athlete by developing different muscles and skills.
6. Girls like baseball players.

I know I was getting desperate with the last one, but his grandmother and great-grandmother both married baseball players. So technically the data was on my side.

But Liam's answer was the same each time.

No.

It's boring. It's too slow. I don't like it. I'm not any good at it. I don't want to play baseball.

After asking him about 500 times, right up to the sign-up deadline, I finally conceded defeat. I had done my best, but it just wasn't gonna happen.

I put my glove away for another season.

A short time later I was driving him home from school when John Lemanski, the St. Angela Athletic Director, called me on my cell phone.

"Is Liam going to play baseball?" he asked.

"No," I sighed. "He doesn't want to. He doesn't like the game."

"Do you mind if I ask him?"

"I've asked him 500 times, and he won't do it," I replied.

"Yeah, but you're a Dad," John responded. "They *like* to say no to you. It might be different if I ask him."

"Hey, he's right here in the car with me," I offered. "Go ahead and try."

I was confident the attempt would be futile. I hoped Liam would let him down easy.

Liam listened for about 45 seconds. They were short of bodies. He could try it, and if he didn't like it, he could withdraw.

"Ok, I'll try it," Liam said cheerfully.

I was stunned.

So all is now right with the world. Liam is playing baseball. He is a third baseman, just like his grandfather, Norbert Switalski, star of *Detroit Catholic Central* and the *Salina Blue Jays*.

We went to Auntie Moe's in Baltimore for Easter, and Liam discovered he likes to bat, so I pitched batting practice and shagged flies with him every day along with his cousins Molly and Andrew and Aunt Moe and Uncle Rick. Liam smoked a few over the fence.

It doesn't get any better than this.

Go Cougars!

May 2006

Life with the British Aristocracy

I give you now *Exhibit One* from the lives of the rich and famous.

The British Open Golf Tournament is being played at Muirfield in Scotland this year. Muirfield is the home of the *Honourable Company of Edinburgh Golfers*, founded in 1744, which makes it the oldest Golfing Society in the world.

Like many hack golfers, it is my ambition to gain entry to the *Company* and its exclusive grounds.

It is, to date, an ambition unfulfilled. I have been kicked off Muirfield more times than I care to mention, but I'll mention two anyway.

It was a sunny Wednesday morning in 1985. I was to be married to my lovely bride, Roma Heaney, in Glasgow two days later. I quickly hatched a plot with my two boyhood chums, Dave Brown and Steve Ratkov, who had crossed the Atlantic to attend my wedding. We decided to drive 60 miles from Glasgow to Muirfield before the wedding and play golf on the famous links. After fighting two hours of Edinburgh roundabouts during the morning rush hour, we presented ourselves at the desk of the Club Secretary, a Captain J A Prideaux, retired officer in *Her Majesty's Royal Navy*.

"You sure we'll be able to get out?" wondered Dave, as our footsteps echoed in the immaculate corridor leading into the Secretary's office.

"According to *Golf Digest*, it's nearly impossible," fretted Steve.

"Quiet, you worrywarts. I'll handle this," I said imperiously. I've known both of them since grade school. They're a couple of *Nervous Nellies.*

"I studied at *Aberdeen University*," I reminded them. "I've played the *Old Course* at St. Andrews half a dozen times. I'm *Scottish*. We'll be fine. You guys just keep your mouths shut."

"*Yes?*" thundered the officious Prideaux from behind his immense oak desk.

"Good morning, sir," I began gamely, hoping good manners would cover my insolent American cheek. "My two colleagues and I have come from the American Colonies in the hope of being granted your permission to play a round of golf at this August Course."

Captain Prideaux eyed us warily as he twisted the curled tip of his waxed mustache.

"When?" he roared.

"It so happens that I am to be married in the fine city of Glasgow in two days time to a red-haired lassie . . ."

"When?" he again interjected, cutting me off.

"Well, we've driven out here this morning . . ."

"When?" he demanded insistently, his voice rising.

I dropped all pretense. "Right here. Right now," I said flatly.

"Never," he said evenly. *"No visitors on a Wednesday."*

"Well, this is our only day to come out . . ."

"Never."

"I've got a stag night tomorrow in Uddingston . . ."

"Never. It is quite out of the question."

I began my retreat in the face of a staccato barrage of *"Nevers"* pouring forth like a bombardment from one of Her Majesty's battleships.

"Okay. I guess that's it then. Thanks anyway. We'll just be going," I whimpered, playing the martyr and hoping Prideaux would relent and show pity.

Nothing doing.

"No visitors on a Wednesday. Never," he continued, as we closed the door softly and shuffled out like three stupefied stooges.

Round one to the *Honourable Company*.

Seven years later, goaded on by my brother Mark, by this time the *Honourable Judge Mark Switalski*, I attempted a second incursion. Having vowed never to cross Claymores with Prideaux again, we based this new assault on the philosophical maxim that *it is easier to seek forgiveness than permission*. We entered the empty clubhouse through the back door, thereby gaining unauthorized entry into the *sanctum sanctorum*.

The walls were graced with enormous oil portraits of *Honourable Brits*, among which I thought I recognized *Dr. Samuel Johnson*. We passed a glass cabinet containing 300-year old wooden clubs, and a *feathery*, one of the legendary original golf balls made of a stitched leather cover stuffed with feathers. There were gutty balls, and mashies and niblicks and spoons, and a magnificent dining room reserved for members, who are required to wear jackets and ties in the clubhouse, and where they can smoke and spit in great comfort.

"May I help you gentlemen?" asked the officer in charge.

"We were just looking for the Club Secretary," I gasped, startled.

"This is *Commissioner Switalski* and I am *Judge Switalski*," interjected Mark. "See here now. Where's that chap *Prideaux*, eh? We don't have our clubs with us but we're determined to sneak in a spot of golf this afternoon," he bluffed, motioning to the empty links.

"I am sorry, gentlemen," the official replied calmly. "But I regret that visitors are not allowed in the clubhouse. If you'll follow me, I'll escort you to the door."

He led us out the service entrance, where my wife Roma was waiting nearby. "You should see inside there," we boasted to Roma. "There's huge portraits, and I cobbed one of these silver spittoons . . ."

The groundsman appeared. "I'm sorry but women are not allowed on the club grounds."

We admired the remaining vistas from the carpark.

Undaunted, bloody but unbowed, I never gave up. 18 years ago, Dave, Steve, Joe Ballor and I founded the *Society of Schoolboys*. Basically it's 16 guys we went to grade school with. The *Schoolboys* stage 2 annual golf tournaments. At the tail end of the 90's boom, we set up an investment fund to save for a future golfing excursion to Scotland. At Steve's keen insistence, we weighted the investments heavily toward tech stocks and energy futures. Enron and the dotComs have not been kind to us, but I recently received excellent news from Britain.

The *Honourable Company* will be pleased to host the *Schoolboys* for golf and lunch in September of 2003.

And my wife can join me for lunch and the 2nd round in the afternoon. Good things come to those who try, and try again.

Britannia Rules!

June 2002

Tam Arte Quam Marte

As San Francisco Giant Barry Bonds approaches Hank Aaron's career homerun mark, national attention is again focusing on steroid abuse. The recent arrest of New York Met clubhouse assistant Kirk Radomski for steroid distribution has widened the scandal that began with the raid on BALCO, the Bay Area Laboratory Cooperative. I have re-introduced SB 30 which would require random steroid testing of high school athletes competing in state tournament games paid for by a $1 surcharge on tournament tickets.

Many of today's athletes are willing to ingest performance enhancing drugs. These include bodybuilders, who eagerly offer their bodies over to steroid experimentation with little regard to the health consequences, professional track and field athletes, and football and baseball stars who seek drugs with one eye on performance and the other on outwitting the testing authorities.

Alas, the latter appears to be surprisingly easy. Until quite recently, MLB did not even regulate steroids, and even the Olympics, with one of the toughest enforcement bodies in international sports, is often no match for sophisticated dopers. Depressingly, the United States has earned an international reputation as a doping hypocrite. While decrying the government-sponsored doping of the East German Olympic team in the 70's and the Chinese team in the 90's, professional sports organizations are among the worst offenders and enablers. Regulation is lax, ineffective, and seems geared toward the protection of pampered athletes. The professional sports and the players unions have been zealous in protecting abusers and keeping testing ineffective. As the case of Barry Bonds demonstrates, no one is willing to turn off the money machine in the name of honest competition.

When the corruption was exposed, the offenders were brought to justice. But sadly, it was justice-lite. Victor Conte and three operators of BALCO were the only individuals who did any time, and they got just 3 months plus probation. The Justice Department worked tirelessly to keep the names of the athletes out of the newspapers. Its only ongoing targets appear to be the authors of the book *Game of Shadows*, who, along with several San

Francisco newspapers, outed the offending athletes by releasing their grand jury testimony in which they admitted illegal drug use.

This leaves us several important questions to ponder. Should the use of performance-enhancing drugs be illegal, and should athletes be rigorously tested? In the absence of self-policing by the governing bodies of athletic competition, should the government impose such rules and enforce them?

My answer is embodied in Senate Bill 30, which I introduced this year..

Clearly the government has a role in protecting the health and welfare of its people, and the American Medical Association has issued clear warnings about kidney damage, depression, and heart ailments resulting from the use of steroids, human growth hormone and other drugs peddled by athletic "trainers." Surveys by the University of Michigan of high school students indicate 5% admit to being users of these substances. And those are the ones who admit it. That is some 20,000 kids nationally.

High school sports are becoming big business. School districts are building large stadiums with artificial turf and multiple gymnasiums. Lucrative scholarships await top players. With the proliferation of weight training in high school sports and the growth of money in the high school level, this pressure on young students to cheat or lose will only grow.

Sports governing bodies show no inclination to police themselves, and the athletes, the people they should be protecting, are only too willing to be guinea pigs. These guinea pigs actively seek out experimental drugs, and pay handsomely for them. Management turns a blind eye to this obvious cheating. Only a Congressional Inquiry, with the threat of government regulation of the sport, caused baseball to take reluctant baby steps toward reform.

Without the press, which leaked the names of the big stars involved, even those steps would never have been taken. But the reporters who pursued the steroid scandal became the villains in the eyes of the players, the owners, and, sadly, for many in the public.

Perhaps the public does not care for honest competition in sports.

We should examine the athletic values of our society. Barry Bonds decided to abandon an honorable career as a Hall of Fame player, arguably the best player of his day, because of the public excitement generated by the 1998 home run race between St. Louis Cardinal Mark McGuire and Chicago Cub Sammy Sosa. Both shattered Roger Maris' 1961 mark of 61 homers, and baseball fans were electrified. Bonds decided to abandon his focus on being a complete player, who could hit, run and field, to become a home run hitter. To add the necessary power, he turned to steroids.

Baseball itself guided this transformation of the game from one of grace and speed and skill to one of pure power, and it is a transformation obvious in other professional sports in America.

It has been a Faustian bargain.

The designated hitter, the smaller ballparks, the emphasis on the home run, and most importantly, the smaller strike zone have changed baseball from a game of skill and strategy to a game of pure power. Despite a rulebook to the contrary, umpires eliminated the high strike, a pitch just below the armpits. That is the hardest pitch for muscle-bound juicers to hit. For many years, weight training was anathema to baseball players because of the loss of flexibility and resulting inability to hit high or inside pitches. Wanting more scoring, and especially home runs, the League and its umpires gradually shrank the strike zone, favoring heavy muscle-bound plodders over smaller but more skilled athletes.

The transformation is just as clear in basketball. Fan enjoyment of the dunk has resulted in players seemingly chiseled from stone replacing smaller players of superior coordination and grace. Officials have relaxed the traveling rules to allow the jump-hop, which allows a player an extra step in order to gather himself for a thunderous dunk and inevitable collision with a defender. NBA small forwards are now 6' 9", and guards are considered small if under 6' 5." Small but lightning fast guards like Tiny Archibald, Muggsy Bogues, Spud Webb, and even Earl Boykins have gone the way of the dinosaur. Basketball is much the poorer for the trade.

Linemen in the NFL will soon reach the 400 pound mark, and football should have the strictest rules regarding drug testing. But it is in the game of golf that the choice between power and skill is most revealing. Players drive the ball further every year, aided by another type of new technology, the equipment revolution in clubs and balls. Professionals now hit the ball so far that classic golf courses that have been played for 500 years must be abandoned or lengthened until they little resemble their former selves.

The changes make the economics of golf more difficult, as more land is required to extend course yardage, the cost of maintenance rises, and reliance on golf carts to cover the distance is more tempting. Golfers hit the ball further but get less exercise. But like baseball and basketball, the essence of the game of golf is not about power.

The motto on the club crest of the Royal Troon Golf Club in Scotland, site of numerous British Open Golf Titles, conveys the essence of the best games: *Tam Arte Quam Marte*: As much by skill as by strength.

That is the lesson that Barry Bonds and the public who supports him have forgotten.

May 2007

Steroid Testing for Student Athletes
Adding sharp fangs to a toothless bill

A toothless bill is better than nothing at all. But it won't take a bite out of steroid abuse.

We finally passed a series of bills to require high schools to adopt a policy regarding steroid use. But the bills don't say what the policy should be, only that the policy must make reference to how steroid use might affect student eligibility. How it might specifically affect student eligibility is left up to the local school district.

I supported the package of steroid bills. These bills represent a modest beginning. But I also offered an amendment because there is so much more we should be doing. I called on the Senate to act vigorously in the defense of our children and in our commitment to integrity.

Those of use who enjoy fair athletic competition got a wake-up call recently with the growing steroid scandal in Major League Baseball. It should be clear to all that this scandal destroys the integrity of athletic competition, invalidates the achievements of individuals, and breaks faith with our ancestors by cheapening the statistical records that are the soul of the game. Steroids rob the health of the athletes who use them and corrupt the youth of our nation by teaching them that:

- Cheating is OK;
- Illegal drugs are good;
- Winning trumps fair play; and
- Although the authorities talk the talk about steroids, they do not have the guts to enforce the rules because they're afraid to rock the boat.

The only way to guarantee fair competition, and protect those athletes who obey the rules from those who cheat and use steroids, is to provide for random testing.

If you think high school steroid use is not a significant problem, then you have your head in the sand. A *Center for Disease Control* report, based on a sample of 15,000 high school students, indicates 6%, <u>or 900 students,</u> had **used** steroids. 900! That is a truly shocking number.

I am disappointed with the *Michigan High School Athletic Association*, which is charged with the responsibility to maintain fair and honest competition in sports and stands as a guardian of our children against overzealous coaches and parents. Why have they not created their own testing program to expel the curse of steroids from the sports they regulate?

I suppose we shouldn't be surprised. The *Association* is as timid as the *Major League Baseball Commissioner* and *Baseball Owners*, who looked the other way for a decade while their sport was horribly corrupted. It took Congressional Hearings, Grand Jury Indictments, and the threat of government intervention to force them to belatedly clean their own house.

My friends, that is the choice we face today.

We have grossly failed our own children if we ignore the abuse of steroids.

I offered an amendment that established random testing for athletes who compete in state tournaments. We would pay for this testing by creating a $1 surcharge on admissions to state tournament games. If we are not willing to fund random testing to police athletics, we are shouting to our children that a dollar is more important than integrity, fairness, and their own health.

We are shouting to them that a dollar is more important than good character.

We are shouting to them that they are saps for being honest and that those who cheat will beat them and get glory and scholarships and wealth and fame. We are telling them that if they want to succeed, they should use steroids too.

Our kids deserve better than that from us.

I cannot believe that this Senate, this State, and this Country would endorse such perversion of our fundamental values.

My amendment failed, 21-17. Two colleagues who voted against me came to me afterward and confided in me that I had spoken well, and that they think I am right, but that we need to build public support first before we mandate testing. Even the committee chair, in arguing against my amendment, conceded that we might have to add testing in the future if these bills are not successful in ending steroid abuse.

The *Detroit News* editorialized against the bills and against my proposal, calling steroid legislation empty gestures against substances few kids use.

I disagree. And so does the state of New Jersey. The same day we passed our bills, New Jersey became the first state in the nation to pass a law mandating random testing, nearly exactly the way I had proposed it for Michigan. Florida is expected to follow suit, and California is not far behind. That same day, baseball pitcher Jason Grimsley, of the Arizona Diamondbacks, had his house raided after he admitted using steroids, amphetamines and Human Growth Hormone (HGH).

He was released by the team the next day.

We owe it to our kids to establish and enforce strict rules about performance-enhancing substances in sports.

The sooner the better.

August 2006

Tales of Johnny McNaught

I still hang out with the guys I grew up with. The golfers among us formed a club 20 years ago, called the "Schoolboys," and we go away for a 3-day golfing weekend every Spring and Fall. We are blessed with tolerant and understanding wives, who also probably enjoy being rid of us every so often.

To commemorate the 20th year of the Schoolboys, we formed an investment club 3 years ago and began saving for a golf holiday in Scotland. By saving early, and riding the market book, we figured we'd live like kings in Scotland.

Our crack financier, Seve, managed our portfolio, investing heavily in energy and tech stocks near the end of the Clinton Boom. After the dust settled on the dot-coms and Enrons, we found that we had less money in the fund than we had put in. We'd be living like kings, all right. Like 10th century kings, without heat or running water and eating gruel.

Attention all Schoolboys! Activate recovery plan!

So we shopped the internet and found cut-rate airfares. And just when we were ready to have Seve hung, drawn and quartered, he totally redeemed himself by surfing the net and getting us into a palatial 7-bedroom townhouse in St. Andrews. The 3-story Georgian was a five-minute walk from the 1st tee on the Old Course, and cost $1850 a week. That's $170 apiece for the 11 Schoolboys who made the trip. *What a bargain!*

We kept the itinerary loose. Some guys wanted to visit distilleries, art galleries, attend soccer games, or try to play as many of the British Open courses as possible. Everyone had something special they wanted to do, but my brother Mark and I were in basic accord.

We wanted to golf our brains out.

To that end, we got off the plane in Glasgow after 18 hours of traveling, drove 5 minutes to Renfrew Golf Club, put on our golf shoes, lifted our clubs onto our shoulders and played 36 holes. We did the same the next day in Lanark and at Cathkin Braes.

I actually had 3 priorities: Golf, drink real ale, and hang out with the locals. Real ale pubs serve a variety of fabulous tasting pints. The beer is so creamy you think you're drinking a milk shake. St. Andrews, a medieval walled town and home of the oldest university in Europe, had a plethora of fine drinking establishments featuring storied ales like Deuchars, Arran, Erdinger, Bitburg, and my personal favorite, Hoegaarden with a slice of lemon.

The pubs were crowded with students and academics and townsfolk who were friendly and eager to talk soccer, politics, culture, and often needed our help with obscure American questions on the nightly pub quiz. I love talking to these people, seeing how they live, or simply enjoying the cadence of their speech.

Playing the British Open Courses is fun, but they are expensive and tend to be played by vacationing foreigners. I have found over the years that the most fun I have is when I play with and against the locals at the courses they regularly play. To this end, I organized a friendly competition against a group of seniors at Cathkin Braes in Glasgow, a private club. We threw 8 Schoolboys in handicapped match play against 8 members, all of whom were retired and most of whom were in their 70's. Each match was worth 3 points. One point for the front 9, one for the back nine, and one for the 18.

They kicked our butts 16 ½ to 7 ½. It was like the tortoise and the hare. The arrogant young Schoolboys were pounding the ball way past the oldsters. But pounding it wildly on occasion, into the gorse and heather. The seniors were straight and steady up the middle. Age and Experience trumps Youth and Stupidity every time. Schoolboy Johnny Boedeker was beaten by an 80-year old man. Whenever I tell this story, and I often do, John immediately chimes in that he took a point in the front and only lost, 2-1. It's not like he got shut out.

Keep telling yourself that, Johnny.

The Cathkin members, as you might imagine, were quite pleased with themselves for humbling the American upstarts. They treated us like Monarchs in the Age of Absolutism, and paid for our golf and pints of ale after the match. We sat in coat and tie in the sumptuous dining room and the Scottish Captain, my friend Danny Cassidy, made a fine speech, welcoming the Schoolboys and thanking us for coming so far and being their guests. He had the grace not to mention us being sacrificial lambs. He also had us all laughing as we licked our wounds from the afternoon's slaughter.

Danny related the story of a friend, a novice golfer, who had played in the pro-am with the great Arnold Palmer. *"Arnie,"* he asked him after the match. "What *one* thing can I do to improve my game?"

Arnold peered at him coolly and offered one word.

"Cheat."

Danny also offered the story of the *Burnside Highlanders Pipe Band*, a popular bagpipe and drum corps in the local Rutherglen area. They had been asked to play at the funeral of a local dignitary, but had been previously booked. In their stead, they offered the services of the Junior Reserve Band, and the family gratefully accepted.

The youngsters had a limited repertoire, but played two numbers that were well received by the mourners. The service was nearing its end, and although gratified by the crowd's approval, the band was somewhat reluctant to finish with the only other song they knew. Nevertheless, as the casket was led out of the Kirk, the band launched into, *"Will ye no come back again?"*

We said our goodbyes and headed East. We enjoyed an epic day with the *Honourable Company of Edinburgh Golfers* at *Muirfield*. The visit took 2 years to set up and featured 36 holes on the Open Course and a fantastic lunch between.

The Schoolboys then settled in for a week at St. Andresws, the *Home of Golf.* Tee times on the *Old Course* are at a premium , and are determined by a daily lottery. On our second day we won the ballot, and everyone was able to play a round on the *Old Course*, the most famous course in the world. Several of us also bought 3-day tickets, permitting unlimited play on 5 other St. Andrews courses for $176. That's $29 a round, *a good bargain.*

The week culminated in a second Ryder Cup, this one against 10 Scottish contemporaries for *The Iron*, the most celebrated trophy in Schoolboy Lore. Various Yank teams have played for *The Iron* four times, and the American team was 1-3 going into this match. This face-off was 9 miles from St. Andrews, in Cupar, and was a 36 hole, handicapped match play competition with team best ball in the morning and singles in the afternoon. John

Martis, the Scottish captain, negotiated bacon rolls for breakfast, soup and sandwiches at lunch and steak pie for dinner, along with 36 holes of golf for the sum of 35 pounds, or $56. *Another great bargain.*

My brother Mark and I faced Captain Martis and Scottish Ace Stuart McGillvray in the morning match. Martis entertained us with tales of *Johnny McNaught*, a mythic associate who had not been chosen for the Scottish team. Johnny had two distinguishing characteristics as a golfer. First, he held his club cross-handed, which resulted in a wicked left hook on every shot. We asked if we could meet *McNaught*.

Martis shook his head. *"He's not available,"* he said flatly. *"But if the Cup is ever played on a circular course running in a counterclockwise direction,"* promised Martis, *"Then Johnny will be selected."*

McNaught's hook was so prodigious, that he aimed every shot far to the right, before his hook brought it back to the left, much like a bowler might. During a round on St. Andrews' Eden Course, Martis dared *McNaught* to aim his tee shot on the 3rd hole far out over the Eden Estuary, a shallow body of water forming the northern boundary of the course.

Johnny accepted the challenge, took a mighty swing, and for the 1st and only time on his golfing career, he sliced the ball right.

"Now Johnny's a bit tight with his money," Martis confided. *"And the tide was out so the estuary was just mud. So Johnny took off his shoes and his socks and waded out about 200 yards thru the muck and got his ball."*

McNaught's second distinguishing characteristic was that he was unable to hit a shot less than 150 yards. This caused him many problems when he attempted to get close to the green. Twenty years ago, when Martis and his pals had just begun playing, their chief ambition was to break 100 on the *Old Course.* One day *McNaught* came to the 18th with his accumulated score at 91. He needed an 8 or better to achieve his dream. After teeing off, he found himself less than 150 yards away. Fearing his erratic swing would sabotage his dream round, he pulled out his putter and croqueted the ball the rest of the way in. After carding a 98, Johnny was the happiest man in the world.

We had great fun in our matches, but at the end of the day the Yanks were conquered again, 15-9. After many pints of ale and speeches, we went home, vowing to return and win back *The*

Iron to its rightful home. Our hosts offered to bring it in two years, when the real Ryder Cup is played at Oakland Hills. We accepted the challenge.

So the holiday ended. I enjoy the game of golf as much as anybody, but the most meaningful and profound experiences of my life are tied to relationships. Playing with my friends and competing against the Scots, enjoying their company and their stories over delicious pints of real ale is what I will remember best and value the most about this fantastic holiday.

Plus Mark and I have developed a new diet. Forget Atkins. All you have to do is play 36 a day, drink as much real ale as possible, and eat whatever you want. Like us, you'll be in the best shape you've ever been and you'll have lost 10 pounds.

October 2003

This Offer Does Not Include Our Wives

Before you get suspicious, let me assure you I worked hard.

I spent my summer in unproductive meetings trying to cut the state's deficit with people who didn't feel empowered to decide the issues. I argued that we should just decide them anyway, and if the leaders didn't like what we came up with, they could reject our recommendation.

After all, I argued, it's easier to ask for forgiveness than permission.

My arguments failed.

So in between meetings, I paid off a debt of my own.

I incurred this debt a year ago playing golf in Scotland.

My brother Mark and I, and pals Greg and John Boedeker entered the **Kelly Open**, at *Fortrose and Rosemarkie Golf Club* way up in the Highlands of Scotland near Royal Dornoch.

Prior to our arrival, Club Secretary Mike McDonald explained the 36-hole alternate-shot tournament was a fundraiser for the local hospice, and asked if we could donate something for the auction that followed the golf.

Greg got a flag from the Buick Open signed by some pros, and someone added a US open golf shirt. As a joke, I offered 2 rounds for 2 people at Gowanie Golf Club in Harrison Twp, along with 2 nights lodging at my house.

At the bottom of the offer, I put in large letters, "TRAVEL TO AMERICA **NOT** INCLUDED."

I figured on no bidders because it was like flying to Paris to get a free lunch.

I begged Greg to bid on my prize, because I didn't want to be embarrassed by a silence among the bidders. "It's worth $100 just in greens fees," I argued.

We'd had a few pints after the first round, and the Guinness and wee nips of scotch whiskey were flowing freely after the second. I may have blacked out for a while. A retired policeman, Jim Tate, acted as the auctioneer, and he would encourage the bidders by frequently repeating in his soft mellifluous cadence, *"Just remember, Lads. It's all for the Hospice."*

The crowd was enjoying itself when Mike got up to introduce the Gowanie package. He was effusive in his praise of how valuable the prize was. I hardly recognized it myself. Perhaps I should have put the travel disclaimer in **Bold Italic.**

When the bidding hit 200 pounds, (about $400) I staggered to the floor.

"I am honored that you would bid on this prize," I said. *"You can stay as long as you want, and play as much golf as you want. I have an extra car, a 2-seat Miata convertible, for your exclusive use."*

When the bidding hit 400 pounds, I got up again,

"Perhaps there is some confusion," I cautioned. *"This offer does not include our wives."*

The crowd roared.

The Guinness kept flowing, supplemented by additional nips of single malt scotch. The bid reached 500 pounds ($1000). Egged on by my brother Mark, who kept feeding me good lines, I got up again.

"OK. The wives are negotiable. But the daughters are off-limits."

After all, it was all for the Hospice.

The spirited bidding ended at 650 pounds, or $1300. Mike McDonald and his pal, Scott Chisholm, were the winning bidders. I was amazed. For a fleeting second, through an alcoholic haze, I considered that perhaps I should have cleared the offer with my wife Roma.

The thought passed quickly.

The rest of the evening was a blur. We couldn't buy a drink, but our glasses were always full, and we were the last to leave the clubhouse. The members insisted we extend our stay and play the locals the next day in a Ryder Cup. One of our playing companions, the silver-tongued Arthur MacArthur, who hailed from the nearby fishing village of Aoch, *(pronounced awk)* prevailed upon his wife to drive us home. We were treated, not just like kings, but like **Rock Stars.** And that was the first day of the trip.

Fast forward a year, to this summer.

The Scots were coming to stay with me for 8 days.

Since I had only known them for a day, and they were *Glasgow Ranger* football fans, my wife Roma asked if I knew whether or not they might be ax murderers.

Not to worry.

Mike and Scott arrived in August, after a couple of days in New York City. Both were around 30, handsome, and single. They were superb gentlemen, Roma loved them, and they were very low maintenance. I am a golfer of meager talents, but Mike is a +1 and Scott a 3 handicap. It was an honor to be in the same foursome with them.

With the help of some friends, I arranged a series of rounds on some of the best courses in the area. My friend Doug Skrzyniarz got them off at Country Club of Detroit, and attorney Lou Corey treated them to 36 holes at Detroit Golf Club.

John Boedeker scalped 7 Tigers tickets against Chicago, with fireworks afterwards, and they loved it. Greg hosted a BBQ featuring 2-inch thick steaks. My pal Chuck Woolaver organized 2 groups at the Orchards.

We played rounds on Katke-Cousins at Oakland University, Forest Akers at MSU with my personal tour of the Capitol and Senate Chambers afterward, and we brought the University of Michigan course to its knees. As the *piece de resistance*, lawyers Greg Buss and Glen Diegel arranged golf at "The Monster," Oakland Hills, the most famous course in Michigan.

For dessert, they got their 2 rounds at Gowanie.

It was hard keeping up with them.

My typical day was to get up at 5 am and stick my newsletter in people's doors till about 10. Then I'd come back and go golfing with them around noon, choke down a few pints in the evening, stumble into bed, and then up again for the lit drop at 5 am the following morning.

Thank God I was able to prevail upon my contacts in the younger generation, including lovely women like Marissa and Vera and Wibka, to show them where people half my age hang out.

They enjoyed the night life in Mount Clemens, Detroit, and Royal Oak.

Mike told me it was the best vacation he has ever had in his life.

We will be returning, God willing, to the Kelly Open in 2011.

Mike says if I offer the prize again, it will go for a minimum of 1000 pounds ($2000).

Because you have to remember.

It's all for the Hospice.

September 2009

Scaling Hadrian's Wall

In 122 AD, the Roman Emperor Hadrian ordered that a wall be built to separate England from Scotland. It seems that the savages of Hibernia were too unruly to be part of the Empire. Barbarians the Scots have remained for two millennia now, as any visitor to a *Glasgow Celtic v. Glasgow Rangers* soccer match can attest.

While we were in Scotland visiting family over the Christmas holiday, my wife, Roma, and I decided it would be good to take a side trip to Hadrian's Wall. I'd always wanted to see it, and it would be educational for our 9-year old son, Liam.

Except Liam didn't come. He spend nearly the entire 3 weeks ensconced in his cousin Neil's loft, playing video games. Upon his return, people asked him what Scotland was like. "You go up a ladder," he explained, "and it's a big square room. They have *GameCube, X-Box, Playstation II and Goldeneye and Super Mario Smash Bothers Melee.* Scotland is awesome."

Cool.

Undeterred, Roma and I struck out on our own, and after a morning drive south from Edinburgh, we crossed the Cheviot Hills and came to the Wall.

The scale of the project is impressive, stretching 72 miles from present day Newcastle to Carlyle. The wall was 15 feet tall and about 8 feet thick, constructed of finished stone by Roman Legions, with a Castle every mile and two watchtowers between each castle. Every 5 miles was a fort with a garrison of 1,000 troops. There were elaborate earthworks in front of and behind the wall, including ditches and mounds to better defend the hinterlands. It's no Great Wall of China, but it's impressive nonetheless.

The remains of the forts reveal elaborate camps with temples and baths, and main streets with fountains and granaries and markets. The buildings had elaborate heating and ventilation systems under the floors, and drains and arches and all the comforts of home. The Roman civilization thrived and villages and towns grew around the forts. The Romans built bridges and depots and roads to administer the Province.

Caesar invaded Britain in 50 BC, and over the next 100 years Rome extended its rule over all of England. But the Romans never succeeded in subduing the Scots. Hadrian's Wall was an admission of the limits of Roman power, and the wall proved effective until the Empire began to crumble in the 4th Century.

The later history of the wall is as fascinating as its origins. Even prior to the final collapse of the Western Empire in 476 AD, Roman provincial rule was disintegrating. When the troops could no longer depend on their pay, they deserted. The Venerable Bede, writing his *History of the English Church and Peoples* in 731 AD, described the dissolution. The British garrison left to defend the wall *"pined in terror night and day, while from beyond the wall the enemy constantly harassed them with hooked weapons, dragging the cowardly defenders down from their wall and dashing them to the ground."*

The wall was still in good condition in Bede's day, but as centuries passed, squatters took possession of the remains of the forts and by the 17th Century the wall was home to brigands and thieves. Amateur historians feared to visit the ruins because criminals controlled the area unchecked. Ironically the wall, built to civilize Britain and keep anarchy at bay, instead became a stronghold for those who preyed upon society and destroyed order. Later local farmers would mine the wall and forest for stones to construct their own houses, barns, churches, and dykes.

The British are reclaiming the wall after centuries of neglect, excavating the forts and uncovering the wall from layers of dirt and the ravages of time. This summer the British Tourist Board will open a hiking path along all 72 miles with buses running the circuit so you can walk the wall at your own pace.

I think that would be a lot of fun.

I've even offered to allow Liam to pull me from the wall with a hooked weapon.

March 2003

The State of Golf in Macomb County

Fore!

Four less, to be exact.

The times they are a-changing for Macomb golfers. Two of Macomb's mainstay golf courses, comprising 54 holes each, are phasing out after many years of existence. Wolverine, at 25 and Romeo Plank, and Partridge Creek, at 19 and Garfield, are in the process of becoming residential housing. Besides these two venerable public courses, tiny TJ's in Macomb Township, a 9 hole operation, is giving way to the inexorable growth of Macomb's northern suburbs. Even private courses are not exempt from the shakeout. Moravian Hills, on Groesbeck in Clinton Township, went public in August before likely going condo in a year or two. Gowanie, in Harrison Township, narrowly averted a similar fate last year.

What's happening?

A bad economy is part of the reason. With unemployment up, overtime down and jobs shaky, people don't have the money to golf. Most greens fees have risen to over $30 per round, and people's disposable income is down. As Sycamore Hills owner Tom Schwark, President of the Golf Course Owners Association of Michigan points out, there's a lot of competition for today's entertainment dollar. The popularity of casinos has emptied a lot of golfers' pockets before they have a chance to go for the real green.

Although Partridge, Wolverine, Moravian and TJs appear headed for closure, there is a new course planned by Cracklewood owner Tom Penzine at 31 Mile, and North Avenue. The City of Troy, in neighboring Oakland County, is preparing to establish a second municipal course near 19 and Dequindre. But Oakland golfers have their own problems. Rochester golf course announced its closure in August.

If you step back and look at what is happening, a pattern emerges. There is now only one golf course south of 14 Mile Road in all of Macomb County, and that is the St. Clair Shores municipal course. This year, the Shorians opened their jewel to non-residents, who can now become members with playing privileges for an annual $50 fee. Gone are Roseville's Sunny Acres, and the GM Tech Center claimed Warren's only course long ago. All that's left of the old course at 10 Mile and 94 in Eastpointe is the Fairway Bar.

With the impending closures of Partridge and Moravian, Clinton Township will be left with only one golf course: Fern Hill. Sterling Heights remains a veritable golf mecca, with 4 courses, Plumbrook, Rammler, Sunnybrook, and Maple Lanes, with its 54 holes.

Macomb Golfers may be facing a longer and longer commute to find a place to play as their old links get developed.

So why is this happening?

Simple. As the county urbanizes, and residential growth moves northward, land becomes increasingly valuable. Farms give way to subdivisions, and golf courses, which often serve as land banks, are no different. Privately owned courses struggling in a tough economy may chose to cash out simply because their land has become so valuable. They may choose to buy cheaper land further north and reopen, or just get out of the business. Cities that want to retain some fine recreational amenities for their citizens may be faced with an expensive proposition if they want to outbid the developers and buy the course. So closure is the most likely outcome.

Golfers might not like this, but the courses are private property, and the owner has a perfect right to sell and develop the land.

So what's a golfer to do?

Governor Grandholm has been talking a lot about cool cities, and livable communities, and our quality of life and how to enhance it. She appointed a task force on smart growth to suggest ways to manage development. A small, but important part of that is finding ways to maintain parks and green space and golf courses to serve the sporting public. Macomb is urbanizing. You can't stop development and I am not sure we would want to. The political question is how to influence, shape, and manage growth.

Macomb still has a lot fine golf courses, but as this year indicates, we could lose a good number of them. For communities already experiencing the boom, the price of land may already be too high. But to the north, far seeing municipalities might be able to purchase marginal or flood plain land to maintain green space and perhaps a golf course for their residents in years to come. They may also wish to negotiate a right of first refusal for courses that exist now. The Huron-Clinton Metropolitan Parks authority did that when they purchased North Brook several years ago. Creative minds may even suggest other alternatives.

Otherwise, can you imagine a day when you have to drive to St. Clair or Lapeer County to get to the nearest course?

January 2004

Off With Their Scalps!

I hope everyone had a sage and wonderful Easter.

As I have for the last 20 years, I went to my sister Monica's house in Baltimore for a long weekend. It is a 500-mile drive through the mountains of Pennsylvania, which my son Liam and I did overnight, arriving at our destination at about 4 a.m. My wife Roma, who does not share our affection for all-night drives, flew out after an important meeting Thursday evening.

We did manage to see the Orioles play the Yankees at Camden Yards. We bought our tickets off a scalper outside the stadium, who proceeded to offer us his cell phone number in case we ever wanted tickets in the future. There is a certain outlaw allure to buying from a scalper. To my 16-year old son, the fact that we bought from a scalper was the highlight of his day.

The Scalping business has changed. I would put it in the general category of behaviors we previously thought of as illegal, and that we now increasingly tolerate. Gambling is an excellent example of such behavior. It used to be outlawed everywhere except Las Vegas, but now we have a plethora of casinos, and many states operate Lotteries.

I am currently in a dispute over advertising the Lottery in the state budget. Operators of the Lottery have asked for an increase in their advertising budget, which they argue will result in increased revenues to the state. All net proceeds, about $700 million, go into the School Aid Fund.

As an aside, that is about 5 percent of the state's $13 billion School Aid Budget. So the most frequently asked question about school funding, "Why do schools need more money? Where did all the Lottery money go?" is best understood by seeing that even with all the Lottery money going to the schools, it is only 5%, or a drop in the bucket.

A good sized drop, but a drop nevertheless.

But I digress.

My argument with Lottery advertising is this: I understand that people are going to gamble, and the state has decided to operate a clean game, away from organized crime, and will devote the proceeds to a worthwhile cause, education. I am on board. But do I have to also spend money to promote gambling?

Are people not gambling enough? Should the state spend money to encourage them to gamble more?

It is one thing for the state to tolerate, and regulate, gambling. It is another matter to promote it. So I offered an amendment to cut the advertising budget last year by 10 percent. I lost that battle. I will probably be content if we just hold the line this year with no increase.

It appears to me that scalping is likewise becoming more tolerable to the public. The fact that the scalper was offering his cell phone number is exhibit one. If you have ever tried to buy Cubs or Yankee tickets on Stub Hub, you have seen exhibit two. Stub Hub is a great website for tickets, and teams used to fight it. Now they advertise it during the games. It is a secondary market for tickets. Like scalping.

Ticketmaster was recently sued by Bruce Springsteen concertgoers, who went on the Ticketmaster website as soon as the concert was announced, yet were quickly moved to a secondary site where tickets were marked up by 100% or more. Ticketmaster settled after being caught for this outrageous form of scalping.

Incidentally, the Orioles, who have suffered through 11 straight losing seasons, are much improved. But they nevertheless lost 11-2 to the Yankees on that day.

I cannot end without detailing the highlights of the trip. We had our 3rd annual McDonnell Family Reunion. My mother, Nancy Ann McDonnell, has a brother Larry McDonnell who lives in the D.C. area, and his family has settled there. Monica started organizing these reunions as a way for us Switalskis to see our aunt, uncles, and cousins on my mother's side.

The centerpiece of these get-togethers, besides a lot of exotic beer drinking, is two competitive events.

The Switalskis stretched their record to 3-0 with a convincing victory in the Switalski v. McDonnell Soccer Match. My 8-year old nephew Elliot scored 2 goals in the win.

That was only a warm up for the main event: Holy Saturday evening's Egg Coloring Contest. With all humility, I must tell you that for the 3rd year in a row, I was awarded 1st prize in the adult division for my rendition of an egg as a can of Budweiser Beer. It had a top and bottom of tin foil over cardboard, with a pop top glued on, and I embossed the top with "Anheuser-Busch." Using pen and ink, I painstakingly drew the label, contents, barcode and other details on the body of the egg.

If I may say so myself, it was brilliant.

The independent panel of judges agreed.

Perhaps you have seen my winner from last year, a dragon emerging from the egg, at the Smithsonian.

Or from two years ago, at the Museum of Modern Art, an egg as the earth, complete with continents.

The Budweiser egg can be seen at my home for a limited time only, before finding a permanent home at the Louvre, in Paris. I understand it will be given the place formerly reserved for the *Mona Lisa*.

April 2009

Policy

Controversial Recall Bill Gains Narrow House Victory

After languishing many months, my wee bill was ready for Prime Time.

An election reform bill I authored was getting a hearing before the House Committee on Redistricting and Elections. Shelby Township Clerk Terri Kowal, Vice President of the Michigan Association of Municipal Clerks, and Roseville Clerk Ron MacKool came to Lansing to testify in support of my bill's modest reform of the filing deadlines for write-in candidates.

Under current law, a write-in candidate can file for office on Friday prior to the Tuesday election.

"That's crazy," MacKool complained. "If you don't know you're running until 3 days before the election, then you're wasting everyone's time."

Clerks generally train their poll workers on the Wednesday and Thursday before the Tuesday election. But if someone files as a write-in on Friday, they have to retrain the staff, on overtime, and redo their tally sheets at the last minute. The Clerks wanted the deadline moved back 3 days, to the Tuesday a week before the election, just prior to their training days.

They had a legitimate issue, so I introduced a bill to fix the problem. While we waited patiently for my bill to be considered, we listened as the Committee took testimony on a Recall bill. This bill required successful recall elections to post at least one more vote to remove an elected official than the number of votes originally cast to elect that person.

Charlie LaSata, a Republican from St. Joseph, was the sponsor of the bill. He testified that one of the townships in his district had 50 recall elections in three years. Township Supervisors were recalled for enforcing the zoning ordinance, which is also known as doing their job. But instead of having a referendum on zoning, the people who opposed zoning organized recalls against the officials who enforced the law.

Kowal and I looked at each other in amazement. Surely this abuse of the recall process should be curtailed. I was particularly outraged by one explanation from an opponent of the bill. "We've had lots of successful recalls," he bragged. "We've won eight out of nine times. We had a problem with one of them because they scheduled it on the same day as the Primary election."

The "problem" was that too many voters came out in the regular "Primary" election. Most voters know about Primary elections. A tiny few know about Special elections. A big turnout in the Primary didn't allow the minority of voters who vote in "special elections" to control the recall.

After several hearings the Recall bill was approved by the Committee and came to the House floor. It went up for a vote, but after about a minute the Republicans "cleared the board." They ended the vote without recording a result because the bill appeared headed for defeat. I liked the bill and I wanted it to pass, so I went over to the Republican side of the aisle to see LaSata.

"Charlie," I asked, "what are they doing with your bill?"

He sat slumped over his desk, with his head in his hands. He had just seen a good three months of work go right down the toilet. "It didn't have enough votes," he said glumly. "It's dead."

"It's a good bill, Charlie," I told him. "I think I can get you some votes on my side."

He perked up. "Really?" he asked. "How many?"

"At least 5 I know of," I told him. "Let me talk to some guys and see if I can get you 10."

I spent the next two hours, between votes and amendments on other bills, talking to colleagues I thought might support the bill. The vote was coming the day after the high profile recall of Flint's mayor, and some members would support the bill, but not so close to the Flint event. They wanted to let things cool down.

I conferred with LaSata. I had 10 votes. We'd try the bill the following week.

"Hey, Mickey," Charlie whispered. "Thanks for your help."

"No problem," I told him. "But do me a favor, Charlie." I took a deep breath and pulled out a copy of my write-in deadline bill. As I blew away the cobwebs the air filled with dust and several large spiders scurried for their lives. "Will you ask the Floor Leader to bring my write-in bill to a vote?"

My bill had waited in obscurity on the Daily Calendar for weeks. The calendar lists all the bills that have passed committee and are awaiting action by the full House. There are about 150 bills on the calendar and only a few get voted upon on any given day. Some never get off the calendar and die an ignominious death at the end of session.

LaSata's Recall bill did come to a vote a week later and passed over the objections of many of my colleagues. In fact, I was the only Macomb legislator of either party to vote for it. But I see it this way. Your vote that you cast in a regular election has to count for something. If you elect someone to do a job for two years, a minority of people shouldn't be able to trump your vote at some special election with a quarter of the regular turnout. And they shouldn't be able to make you stand guard for 2 years, and have to go out again to the polls on some random date to defend your original vote.

You voted someone in for a term of office. Unless they have committed a crime or screwed up royal, your chance to replace them is at the end of their term. If you don't like their judgments or policies, vote them out at the next regular election.

The nation as a whole agrees. Recalls aren't even a generally recognized right. 20 states don't even allow them, and of the 30 that do, 15 restrict recalls to malfeasance. Only 15 of the 50 states provide for recalls for any reason, like Michigan does.

I voted for LaSata's bill, and got others to vote with me, because I thought it was a good bill. I didn't care that he was a Republican and I was a Democrat. The Macomb Daily agreed, editorializing that I *"should be applauded for being the only Macomb County state representative to back [the] legislation . . . [while] 7 of the 8 Macomb House members took the politically correct path by opposing a bill that places an added burden on the recall activist. Only Switalski supported the will of the majority by strengthening the rules on recall elections."*

My write-in bill passed about a week after LaSata's. Neither one has yet come to a vote in the Senate. We have until December 31st to get them into law, because all unpassed bills die at the end of the 2-year session. We'd have to start all over again in committee next year.

Wish us luck. Or try to recall us while you can.

Note: LaSata's bill died in the Senate. After five years and two re-introductions, my bill finally passed in 2006.

March 2002

You Have Nothing to Lose but Your Chains
Legislature Considers Changes to Item Pricing Law

In the 10,000 years since Neanderthals left the cave, man has erected a complex civilization conducting global commerce according to fair rules of trade instead of piracy and the law of the jungle.

But don't be fooled.

That thin line between order and chaos is only a *mismarked box of Cocco Puffs* away. One of my House colleagues has put civilization at risk by offering a bill recently to eliminate some provisions of Michigan's *Item Pricing Law*, arguing that the law is burdensome to retailers.

He's playing with dynamite. Michigan's law is very popular with consumers. It is well-understood and frequently invoked by savvy shoppers.

The law's provisions are simple. Items in stores must be individually marked with a price sticker. If an item is scanned at checkout with a higher price, the retailer owes you the difference, plus 10 times the difference, up to a maximum of $5.

The law makes shopping more convenient, so you know what things cost and don't have to run around checking prices all day. But even more important, the *Item Pricing Law* is your secret weapon in the guerilla war against insensitive corporate giants. OK, so they make your life miserable with phone solicitations during dinner, send you incorrect electronic billings which can't be corrected until your credit history is ruined, and then downsize you after leaving you with a pension full of worthless company stock.

But *you* can bring *them* to their knees with the *Item Pricing Law*. And if you don't fancy your odds against Corporate Giants like *MicroSoft*, the *Item Pricing Law* is still the ultimate trump card against rude store staff.

It's a jungle out there. I thought the uneasy truce between shoppers and store clerks only broke down in the final hours before Christmas. But the truth is the war is waged daily in the trenches of suburbia. Even if you already knew the job of a store clerk was difficult, I'll bet you haven't guessed the half of it.

Some time ago my friend Dave suffered an outrage at a local video store. It seems that his video game, which he admittedly returned a few hours late, was automatically rented for another week at a cost of $25. He didn't want it for another week. Couldn't he just pay a late fee?

"No, dude," mumbled the cashier through the decorative metal post adorning his tongue. "The computer's already charged you. It's automatic. That's, like, the rule, man."

"That's absurd!" responded Dave man. "What's more important: Man or the Machine?"

An appeal failed when the manager backed the Machine. Furious, Dave cut short his argument and turned to his daughters. "Let this be a lesson to you," he lectured the stunned children. "Don't you ever treat a customer this way. This is how you lose a customer and make them never come back to you!"

He continued his tirade loud enough for the whole store to hear. Every eye in the place stared as he marched out of the store with his crimson-faced daughters in tow. True to his word, Dave has not returned in 4 years.

Dave's boycott works on a purely negative level, but the resentment smolders. As an instrument of satisfactory revenge, the *Item Pricing Law* is infinitely preferable. It provides the opportunity to get Big Business where it hurts. So aggrieved shoppers plot their revenge carefully.

My friend Veronica had a disagreement with an automobile accessories establishment some time back. At issue was an overcharge. A self-described expert on the item-pricing law, the wily Veronica wielded the law like a stilleto.

Eyeing the overcharge, she remained calm, seemingly oblivious to the miscarriage of justice being perpetrated upon her. Eagerly she offered full payment upon presentation of the fraudulent bill. She thanked the representative of Big Oil profusely for their services. She then pocketed her change and took the receipt.

Instantly she was transformed into a demon. "You have overcharged me for the rear-view mirror hanging red foam dice," she announced triumphantly. "They are marked $3.79 and you charged me $4.59. By law you owe me the difference plus 10 times the difference.

You are indeed fortunate that the Michigan Legislature took pity on charlatans like you and provided a maximum. I want my $5."

The cashier was new to the job, and excused herself to consult the manager. She returned shortly with an excuse. The manager was busy.

Veronica had had enough. "That's it!" she stormed. "I want my $5 now or I'm going to chain myself to the front door of this establishment with a sign that says you are a cheater."

Her husband surreptitiously contacted the manager. "You'd better give her the five bucks," Randy warned him. "She's got the chains in the trunk. She'll be back in half an hour wearing a helmet with horns and a leather bodice."

Veronica was disappointed when the manager cracked and surrendered the fiver. "Some things are *just worth* going to jail for," she vowed eagerly.

Some people have used the *Item Pricing Law* to supplement their income. My friend Joannie was laid off recently, and she is a dedicated *"Michigan Bounty"* hunter. "I pick up $5 to $10 a week, easy," recounts Joannie. "What the heck—it's my spending money while I'm laid off."

For a bounty hunter, Joannie is amiably direct. "If I were you," she counseled a cashier as she collected on an overcharge, "I'd change those price stickers on the PEZ dispensers right away. Otherwise, I'll be back tomorrow for another $5."

It is true that the *Item Pricing Law* cannot rectify every injustice. It was of no use in the mother of all floorfights, the *Instant Pizza Affair* several years ago between Helena and the Customer Service Rep at *Major Cheese's Kingdomland*. Helena took my son Liam and his pal Ricky out to play video games and eat lunch. She had just bought 50 tokens and ordered a large pizza, when she changed her mind.

"Wait," she interjected. "Make that a medium pizza."

"I'm sorry," the waitress replied. "The large pizza's already ordered."

"No, no," Helena replied patiently. "I've just now ordered it. I want to cancel it."

"It's too late. You ordered it."

"I just ordered it 15 seconds ago! This is ridiculous! I want to speak to the manager."

When the manager refused to budge on the quick order, all pretense of civility broke down. Helena mumbled an unflattering characterization of the manager, and the manager offered to refer the matter to the city's uniformed personnel. For a moment Helena considered an exploratory incision in the woman's jugular, but 6-year old Ricky was tugging at her jacket, pleading, "Let's just go home." Liam, who knows his aunt better, was putting his tokens on Helena. But in deference to innocent youth, and since the woman appeared to be a bleeder, Helena accepted the indignity of being banned from Chuck E. Magic's Kingdomland.

And that's the way it is. Score it *Merchants 2, Consumers 2.* Shoppers already have it tough enough out there. I don't think it's a good time to weaken the *Item Pricing Law.* Some things are *just worth* going to jail for.

February 2002

Why Can't We Cut?
Can Macomb Survive with Fewer Judges?

A couple of months ago, the Chair of House Appropriations laid down a challenge to all legislators. He said if anyone had any ideas about how to reform government, now was the time to bring them forward.

I accepted this challenge.

The next day I made a budget savings proposal to my colleagues. I suggested that we could begin downsizing government by not filling Circuit Court judicial vacancies when a judge turns 70 and can no longer run for re-election. Current law allows judges who turn 70 to finish their terms, but they cannot seek re-election. I figure with no incumbent, no one was losing a job, and that by attrition, we could begin to downsize the judiciary to a level we can afford.

It is clear to me that Michigan Government has to get smaller, and since there are 9 such judicial vacancies around the state in 2010, this would be a great time to begin. Each judge costs the state about $140,000 in wages, so cutting out 9 would save the state over $1 million. More importantly, at a time when we are cutting revenue sharing payments to counties, each judge costs the county about $1 million, so the counties would save about $9 million.

The following week, by chance, we were doing the Judiciary budget in the Senate, so I took advantage of the opportunity to introduce my amendment to the budget, saying that at the discretion of the SCAO (the State Court Administrator's Office), and the affected County, that the state could delay filing judicial vacancies created when judges aged out of the system.

I showed my amendment to the Republican Floor Leader, who also chairs the Judiciary budget. He liked it immediately, and agreed to support its passage. My amendment passed easily on a voice vote.

Two of these 9 vacancies are in Macomb County, were two Circuit Judges are ineligible for re-election in 2010. Macomb County has a budget deficit of $15 million, and that is *after* they raised taxes. So clearly the County must make some cuts, and this is an excellent place to start.

Some opponents to my proposal argued that we should cut judicial salaries or eliminate unspecified probate judges. They did not put these suggestions into the form of an amendment. Nevertheless, Senate Republicans agreed to remove my amendment the following day, on a party-line vote.

"Where are my fiscally responsible Republican friends?" I asked my colleagues. I hope they will eventually change their minds. This is a concrete chance to cut government to the size we can afford, which all fiscally responsible legislators, both Republican and Democrat, agree must be done.

I remain hopeful that my proposal will become law.

I believe some of the opposition rests on personal reasons. It is widely believed that siblings or offspring of the retiring judges would have a good chance of winning an election succeeding their namesake. Let me go on the record saying I like those individuals and I consider them my friends.

But whether they might win an election is no basis for making budget choices. It should have nothing to do with it.

In any rational system, the decision to fill vacancies should belong to those people paying the bill. In this case that's the counties ($9 million) and SCAO ($1 million). Shouldn't they have the ability to say whether they want to fill openings, or delay filling them for 2 years so they can save money and balance their budgets? Shouldn't this *always* be their option?

The Chief Judge of the Macomb Circuit Bench is strongly opposed to my proposal. He has been quoted on the Senate floor and in the *Macomb Daily* as saying Macomb should have 5 more judges. I believe this is a fundamental misunderstanding of economic reality in the wake of the bankruptcy of GM and Chrysler. We have the highest unemployment in the nation. We can not grow government – we have to shrink it.

We can't fix Macomb County's $15 million deficit by spending $5 million more for new judges. We have to reduce government to what we can afford. It is abundantly clear that we can't afford the 13 judges we already have. The Board of Commissioners has asked the Circuit Court to cut their budget by $900,000. If they can't get savings by not filling vacancies, then they will have to give workers unpaid furlough days or lay off 20 Friend of the Court clerks, child support investigators, referees, and other employees who actually make the Court function on a daily basis.

The Chief Judge suggested to the *Macomb Daily* that the 2 year delay in filling these positions would only save $40,000 by eliminating a secretary. I don't know how he came up with that number, but my figures come from estimates made by the County Finance Director, the man who does the budget numbers for a living.

And he says each judge costs close to $1 million when you add up the costs of the Secretary, County Clerk, Court Recorder, Court Officer, 2 Prosecutors, and all the operational costs.

There are 13 judges on the Macomb Circuit Bench, and they held a vote on my proposal. Eight of them support delaying filling the vacancies for at least 2 years. One was absent. That left 4 opposed. The Macomb Board of Commissioners, who are the budgetary authority, voted 23-3 in support of my proposal.

I try to make decisions that are good for the state. All I am saying is let the people paying the bill decide whether they can live with fewer judges. If they believe they can, they should be allowed to reduce government. This concept is supported by the State Court Administrators Office, the Michigan Judges Association, the Michigan Association of Counties, the unanimous vote of Oakland County Circuit Court (which also has 1 such vacancy), Republican County Executive L. Brooks Patterson, and the majority of the Macomb Circuit Bench. Wayne County Prosecutor Kim Worthy has likewise asked the Governor to not bill vacancies on the Wayne Bench.

This isn't rocket science. So why hasn't it been adopted?

'Cuz cutting, like breaking up, is hard to do.

September 2009

Macomb Settles for Half

It went down to the wire, but Macomb County got its top legislative priority the last night of the 2009 session in Lansing.

After 6 months of wrangling in the State Senate, I was finally able to overcome Republican opposition and gain passage of a bill allowing Macomb and Oakland Counties to reduce the number of judges on their respective Circuit Court Benches.

The bill was supported by the Macomb County Board of commissioners, 23-3, and by the County Judges, 11-4. and although the State House passed it overwhelmingly by a 97-4 vote, the opposition of Senator Alan Sanborn (R-Richmond) nearly killed it for both counties.

Rather than see the bill die, I offered a compromise. Oakland got exactly what they requested, but I agreed to only cut one Macomb Judge instead of two. I did extend the period before the seat would be filled again from 2 years to 6 years.

So instead of Macomb delaying 2 judges for 2 years, we will delay filling 1 judgeship for 6 years. We will save $3 million over 6 years, instead of $2 million over two years. There is a time value to money, so don't get too excited. But the legislation does shrink government and save money.

Macomb and Oakland are struggling to balance their budgets. They approached legislators about not filling Circuit Court judicial vacancies when a judge turns 70 and can no longer run for re-election. Oakland wanted to delay filling one of its vacancies for 4 years, and Macomb requested permission to delay filling 2 vacancies for 2 years each.

I thought the request made sense, and fought hard for passage for over 6 months. We had strong political support from the Oakland Bench, Commission and Executive L. Brooks Patterson. We had strong editorial support from The *Macomb Daily*, which called it "refreshing," and the *Detroit Free Press*, which praised its "innovative thinking." It had the support of watchdog groups like Taxpayers United Michigan, whose Chairman, Bill McMaster, championed its cause. Other organizations like the Michigan Association of Counties, Michigan Judges Association, and the State Court Administrator's Office lent their endorsement.

Despite all this support, the bill was blocked in the Senate by Sen. Sanborn. His opposition could not stop the Oakland bill from passing the Senate, but he was able to kill the Macomb portion. His Republican colleagues were willing to give him the benefit of the doubt regarding conditions in Macomb. They took his word that the bill would not save money, despite a detailed estimate provided by Macomb County Finance Director Dave Diegel, which matched Oakland's estimate. And they believed his assertion that the cuts would create a backlog, despite a similar backlog in Oakland County and the recommendation of both SCAO and Judge Ken Sanborn, the Chief Judge of Probate, that one judge could handle the Probate Court and a 2nd judge could be reassigned to Circuit to lower caseloads.

I believe the key to passage was the willingness of Macomb's advocates to compromise and offer to cut only one judge instead of two. While this did not convince Senator Sanborn to vote for the bill, I believe it caused the rest of his colleagues to evaluate the bill on its own merits, instead of deferring to his judgment.

Since we were willing to compromise, we appeared to be more reasonable. Contrary to popular opinion, legislators don't like to fight. If they feel that one side is being intransigent, and is not negotiating in good faith, they will reward the compromising party with their vote.

In the end, the compromise passed the Senate 31-1, with Senator Sanborn being the only Senator in opposition to the bill. The House ratified the agreement 95-7.

I am disappointed we were not able to cut two judges, because I think our proposal was logical, our budget situation is grave, and that is what both Macomb's Judges and Commission were asking for. I am sorry I could not deliver the full savings.

But it was the best we could do. And in the legislature, half a loaf is better than none.

October 2009

Water, Water, Everywhere

I got a call from the late, great Tom Welsh a few years ago. I was just a lowly County Commissioner, and Tom was a legend in local politics, one of the larger than life figures that built Macomb County.

Tom wanted to have lunch. I couldn't figure out what he would want with a punk like me. I guess he saw something in me, and figured I might be headed somewhere some day. We sat down to eat. Tom talked about the construction of the drain system and the hurdles Macomb County faced during the postwar years when the suburbs were rapidly expanding.

I could certainly relate to his tales. I remember growing up on Fountain Street, in Roseville, where every summer rainstorm brought a flooded basement. My mother would wait by the basement floor drain to sound the alarm, and my dad and the men of the neighborhood would spring into action, lifting washers and dryers up onto wooden boxes, moving from house to house to save basement valuables.

That routine largely ended when the drain system was installed. Tom had played a central role in the creation of that system, and he was justly proud of the fact. He also had a strong interest in seeing the system succeed.

He told me that intermittently issues regarding the Detroit Water & Sewerage Department might come up. He said that he did not favor *Regionalization,* a transfer of ownership of the system from Detroit to the Metropolitan Area. He cited a number of complex technical reasons for this. But he urged me to always keep one principle in mind. Since the suburban communities made up 75% of the users, they deserved some measure of representation and control on the Water Board that governs the system.

I've always remembered that conversation. Regionalization bills have been around for a decade, but up to now they've never gone anywhere.

This year may be different. Water has become a big political issue, partly because of Lake St. Clair pollution, but mostly because of rising water bills. Water has become an issue in several political campaigns. Warren City Attorney George Constance has made it a major issue in his campaign for Macomb Circuit Court.

Gubernatorial candidates Grandholm and Posthumus have sparred over the issue. Warren has even sued Detroit to get the rate formula.

Clinton Township Republican Leon Drolet introduced a bill to regionalize the water system back in March, but the bill was ignored until the heat of campaign season. When the bill was first introduced, I went around to all my Macomb County Democratic colleagues in the House and told them I was going to cosponsor the bill. Normally Democrats would not sign onto a controversial Republican bill.

After all, the bill would inflame the Detroit delegation, splitting my colleagues and dividing the caucus. Some suspected the bill wasn't designed to solve a problem, but would only serve to further divide and alienate city and suburb. I considered those drawbacks, but I signed on anyway, because I believe some changes short of full regionalization are justified. All 8 Macomb representatives ended up cosponsoring the bill.

The interests of the suburban communities are simple. What we are talking about is the public water supply. The suburbs make up 75% of the users of the system, and we want some control over its governance. There have been a lot of charges of mismanagement and failure to collect unpaid bills leading to rate increases. At bottom Macomb wants to be sure everyone is paying their fair share. We don't want to be subsidized, and we don't want to subsidize other communities.

I think those are reasonable demands.

But even during the heat of a campaign, sometimes it's useful to listen to what the other guy says. You might learn something, and you might even stumble onto a solution. Detroit says that its water is among the safest and cheapest in the country. It says the suburban communities blame Detroit for increases, when it's really them adding surcharges onto what they pay Detroit, marking up bills by 100%, 200%, or even more than 300%. Finally, Detroit says they paid for, own and operate the system. We are their customers. If we want to own and run the system, we can buy it from them.

For $2 Billion.

Otherwise they'll see us in court.

Gulp.

When the shouting is over and the steam clears, I think two specific changes are in order. First, the rate structure should be public. Every community should be able to see how everyone's rate is calculated and ensure we all are paying our fair share. And if that hasn't been happening, some adjustments are in order.

Secondly, Macomb, Oakland, and suburban Wayne currently each have a representative on the Water Board. But that person is appointed by the Mayor of Detroit. At the least we should be able to appoint our own representative. Our representative will ensure our interests are brought to the table when policies are adopted.

If we accomplish these two objectives, I believe we will have improved the system.

And I think Tom Welsh would feel we have done a good job.

November 2002

Detroit Water Politics Leave Us All Wet

You would be shocked by two actions, taken by the Legislature since our last E-Insider, that defy all logic and proportion. Both actions involve the Detroit Water and Sewerage Department, and maybe that explains a lot.

When suburbanites hear "Detroit Water," many suspect that the City is about to raise their water and sewer bill. Many suburbanites distrust the City and often expect the worst. Suburban politicians know this, so some use the City as a punching bag. But last week they looked like Joe Frazier, who used to punch himself as he chased his opponent.

A lot of leaders who should know better have made a good living out of bashing Detroit. That's too bad. But I didn't get into politics to exploit people's suspicions and fears, so I won't support legislation that might sound good to you as a headline, but that would cause useless division and waste your money in reality.

Which brings me to the two actions of the past two weeks.

Detroit Mayor Kwame Kilpatrick and the Detroit Water and Sewerage Department recommended a 6% increase to water rates recently, and requested that the new rates be approved by the Detroit City Council. No one likes paying more for water, but Detroit's water is among the nation's best in terms of cost and quality. In a normal world the increase probably would have been accepted, with some grumbling, and we would have gone on to the next issue.

Instead, the Detroit City Council approved the rate increase for the suburbs, but left Detroit customers' rates unchanged.

That illegal, unjust and foolish action unleashed a barrage of well-deserved criticism. Suburbanites were justifiably outraged. Mayor Richard Notte of Sterling Heights and I were in Lansing the next day, and questioned the City of Detroit's lobbyist on how the Council could have done such a dumb thing and how we suburbanites would not tolerate it. He apologized and assured us that the decision would be reversed the next day.

It was.

For the second time in a row, the first being their embarrassing blunder on the Detroit Zoo, the Council had to quickly reverse itself and adopt the Mayor's original proposal. You would think that only a political genius could convincingly portray Kwame Kilpatrick as a wise and reasonable leader to suburbanites, but the Detroit Council did it twice in a week.

But Lansing elevated this comedy to a farce.

The Legislature immediately passed a law to create a Suburban Board to oversee the Detroit Water Department. Proponents claimed that now the department would be run fairly and efficiently. At least that is how the headlines described it.

But the actual language in the bill was quite different.

The "Board" created in the bill was actually an "Advisory Board" with no power to approve, disapprove, modify or reduce any water rates. So the Board had no power to do anything about water rates. Yet the bill also permitted the Advisory Board to hire an executive director and a staff.

In other words, the solution this bill proposed was to create another powerless bureaucracy with no control over water rates. In fact, passage would result in higher water bills, because users of the system would now have to pay for an additional powerless layer of state government.

I know many people dislike Detroit, but I don't think their feelings have blinded them to the extent of wanting to hire a useless bureaucracy to advise us that rates are too high.

We already know that. But the bill passed anyway. Thank God the Governor will veto it.

The second piece of nonsense was a resolution to request a Federal Judge to force the Mayor of Detroit to submit Water Department contract documents to the Detroit City Council rather than to continue submitting them to the Judge.

Now just ask yourself: Would you go out of your way to replace a Federal Judge's oversight with oversight by the Detroit City Council? Would you do this after the Council had just committed historic blunders in decisions made on the future of the Detroit Zoo and on establishing water rates in the City and suburbs?

There are sensible things we could do. If you think about it, the water should belong to the public. No one can own it, and Detroit can only manage the system so long as they manage it in the best interests of all of the users. If they ran it to benefit themselves at the expense of the other users, we would be justified in taking management of the system away, after just compensation. But at present, we should reform the existing Water Board. Each of the suburbs, including Macomb, has a seat on the Board. But that seat is appointed by the Mayor of Detroit. We don't even get to appoint our own representative!

Surely Macomb should be able to appoint its own representative.

My bill to accomplish this has languished in the Senate for years.

Instead we pass bills to create powerless bureaucracies and give more power to the Detroit City Council.

Go figure!

March 2006

Code Red in the Emergency Room

I don't like going to the doctor's.

But I wanted to understand the problems in health care, so I decided to spend some time with doctors in hospital emergency rooms. Most sane people wouldn't willingly spend time there, but I figured that was part of the job you elected me to do. Just like visiting prisons.

You don't want to go there, either.

With the cooperation of St. John's, Beaumont, and Detroit Medical Center (DMC), I arranged to spend 3 Friday nights, from 10 pm to Midnight, with the staff in the Emergency Rooms of each hospital. I began Halloween Night, after the trick or treating was over and my son was in bed. I figured if I survived the first two without passing out, I would work my way up to Detroit Receiving, which I did in February.

I suppose if I was really dedicated, I'd have made my visits on nights with a full moon between 1 and 3 am after the bars close. But even my curiosity and desire to serve the public has its limits.

Anyway, I started out at St. John's Hospital on Halloween night. There was a lot of action. I saw things that made me appreciate what doctors and nurses and staff have to go through every day. Later, I got the suburban perspective by visiting Troy Beaumont, and concluded with visits to Hutzel Women's Hospital, Children's Hospital, and Detroit Receiving, all part of the DMC.

It was an education I won't forget.

The Attending Physicians run the Emergency Rooms. The ones I met had the patience of Job. The men and women I spent time with kept their heads when all about them were losing theirs. They were well organized, and utilized state of the art technology to fight illnesses. I watched in wonder as doctors at Beaumont monitored a screen with real time results of blood tests and MRI images as we searched a patient's internal organs for a kidney stone.

I saw a baby born 15 weeks premature at Hutzel, just over a pound, with a head the size of an apricot. She was on a ventilator in an incubator and was being cared for by a dedicated and loving staff. And there were 14 more like her.

I saw great teamwork.

The physician at St. John's introduced me to a bright young woman who was the resident, one of the graduate medical students who work long hours for relatively low pay and keep the system working. She ran through the case histories of about 8 patients in each successive cubicle and her diagnosis of each. The attending physician gave her feedback on each case and then followed up personally, beginning with the most difficult cases. They made an impressive pair.

It can get wild at times.

Just when I was getting comfortable an ambulance radioed ahead with a critical case. An elderly woman had a window shattered onto her as she lay in bed. She was breathing with great difficulty, and had a Do Not Resuscitate (DNR) order.

A team of six doctors, nurses and respiratory specialists prepared quickly for her arrival, all the while trying to determine what to do about the DNR order. Was it verbal or written? Was it properly executed? Would a family member be present? These tough questions would have to be answered in minutes.

And you see all kinds of things. Prisoner care is provided at Receiving, and it's routine to see policemen and prisoners in emergency. At St. John's I met a cop waiting there to question a woman who had been set on fire by some trick or treaters.

Even the patients can be difficult.

One man with a substance abuse problem and a plastic neck brace on was shouting that he wanted someone to get him the #&*@ out of there. The attending physician went over and quietly calmed him down. He explained to him why they needed him to lie still for a while to get lab results on his condition. He relaxed, and said he understood and thanked the doctor. Before the doctor had taken three steps away from him he was up again, shouting to be released.

Once we were called to the front desk to answer a complaint. One of the men in the waiting room had grown impatient. He'd gone outside for a smoke. In the meantime he had been called, searched for, and couldn't be found. The staff went to the next patient. He returned later and became irate. He punctuated his dissatisfaction by smashing a pumpkin in the lobby, and left again.

You see things that are wrong with our society, or that are inefficient, or that there are no easy answers to.

I saw an elderly couple, in their 80's, with no health insurance. They had no family doctor, so the emergency room was their primary care provider. The wife was in because she was listless and not responding. She and her husband can't drive, so they arrived by ambulance, which is expensive. Her condition is chronic, meaning it's not really going to change. She was dehydrated and suffering from malnutrition. The staff made her comfortable and put her on an IV drip. Her husband sat silently by her bedside. They would go home, again by ambulance, in a few hours. They had been in the week before for the same problem.

This surely isn't the most efficient way to deliver health care services. Emergency Room care is expensive because it is there, 24/7. But the elderly couple didn't seem to have an alternative.

"That isn't especially burdensome," a doctor explained. "We're already here, set up to provide care, and we can prioritize cases. If someone with a chronic problem has to wait 15 minutes while we deal with a crisis, they usually accept that."

Far more frustrating is the case of another 80 year old. She was in the emergency room 10 days earlier because of an infection. She was treated, given a prescription for antibiotics, and sent home. When she went to the pharmacy, she couldn't afford the $80 cost of the prescription. She didn't take the antibiotics, the infection grew worse, and she began vomiting with toxemia. This time she had to be admitted to the hospital.

Now she will receive the drugs as a hospital patient.

"We try to be very sensitive to our patients on fixed incomes with limited ability to pay," a resident told me. "We do our best with free samples, and try to prescribe the lowest cost alternatives. But there is only so much you can do."

These are difficult financial times for most hospitals. The DMC has particular challenges because 30 percent of their patients have no insurance and no money. By law the hospital must treat anyone who enters their doors, but they get no compensation for nearly a third of their patients. Another 30 percent are Medicaid patients, whose reimbursement rates are so low that hospitals lose money on most cases. The DMC is like the car salesman that put prices so low that "I lose $100 on every car I sell. But I make it up on volume."

The DMC expects to lose $52 million this year

Even with Medicare reimbursement rates at such a low level, there is a gaping hole in the state's Medicaid budget. Governor Granholm has proposed a 75 cent a pack cigarette tax increase to raise $300 million to help fill that hole. I voted against the last increase, but this one is an especially tough vote. It's hard to see how hospitals with a disproportionate share of Medicaid patients would function without the Medicaid program. We could throw 200,000 more people off Medicaid, but besides being cruel, that would only increase DMC's totally uncompensated care.

Clearly, legislators opposed to the cigarette tax need to identify a solution to the $450 million shortage.

Four years of financial stress have taken their toll on many medical services. The doctors at Children's Hospital mentioned some of the serious problems they have with untreated dental problems in children, and I recalled with consternation cuts we were forced to make in dental care for handicapped children in last year's budget.

I thought about recent proposals to cut funding subsidizing the wages of medical students and shuddered to think what the system would run like without them. We get a lot for our money.

One bargain I saw involved a man in a motorcycle jacket who got in a fight and was hit across his forehead with a metal bar. The sizeable gash was stitched together by a fourth year med student, who had a knack for sewing.

Perhaps he'd worked his way thru med school as a tailor. His patient was in remarkably good spirits for just having been bludgeoned. As soon as he'd finished, the student was asked it he wanted to try his hand at another. He happily agreed.

"We'll keep him busy all night," the attending physician winked at me.

In spite of the economic difficulties, all the hospitals provided excellent care delivered by conscientious employees. They even found ways to make lemonade from lemons. The attending physician at Receiving pointed out with pride that their trauma unit had unique advantages in being able to give some of the quickest and best care. Many of their patients come to them without insurance or their own physician. So the trauma unit isn't hamstrung by having to worry about getting HMO or insurance company approval or consulting with personal physicians. "We can diagnose you and complete surgery on you in a couple of hours," a surgeon joked.

"You'd better watch out," I warned the director. "The other hospitals will complain that the only reason you can see patients quicker is because you don't have to mess with insurance paperwork."

"We'd be happy to exchange payer mixes with those hospitals," he grinned. "We'll even put in a high speed copier to make an impression of those insurance cards."

We've had four years of surgery and multiple amputations on the state budget. No one can say we haven't done a lot of cutting. The state has 8000 fewer employees than we did in 2001, our employees work 2 hours every week without pay, and we let 150 prisoners out of jail in Macomb County the last 2 months of 2003. And we are still $1 billion in debt.

We need to be careful.

Additional cuts to the health sector could pull the plug on our life support system.

March 2004

Ethanol is the 85% Solution
BioFuels Are the Key to Jobs and Economic Recovery

It's been a long hot summer.

Jobs are in short supply, and gas prices have settled in at about $3 per gallon. Michigan needs a plan to create jobs and control energy costs. The answer is right in front of us.

We can control our destiny by our own actions. Gas prices are high, and they could go higher. Unemployment is unacceptably high. But we can create jobs and bring down gas prices by a combination of making some wise investments and altering our behavior.

Rather than complain about the cost of gas, let's get even. Big Oil is riding high. They literally have us over a barrel. Exxon Mobile earned a record $36 billion in profits and gave its retiring CEO a $400 million bonus. It's time we tamed Big Oil.

How?

Rather than repeat the gridlock arguments about windfall profit taxes, $100 rebates, or repeal of gas taxes, all of which are incredibly bad ideas, the easiest thing to do is reduce our consumption.

There are several ways to do this, the easiest way is to simply slow down. I drive to Lansing three times a week, and that's a 200-mile roundtrip. I drive a Saturn, which normally gets 36 miles per gallon. I used to average 73 mph, but now I hold steady at 60. And my gas mileage improved to 41 mpg.

That means I save nearly $4 per fill-up. And I am contributing to lower national consumption, which will increase supply and lower demand, meaning less upward pressure on prices.

My point is that we consumers of energy are not powerless. We play a significant role.

Other ways to save include buying a more fuel-efficient vehicle. Consumers are doing this in droves, but unfortunately the Big 3 have been caught with a mix of 8 mpg Hummers and SUVs and have paid the price in lost market share.

We faced similar issues in the late '70s after OPEC, the oil cartel, jacked up the price of oil. We prevailed in the 80's by getting more efficient in our use of oil, reducing demand, and expanding production.

We can do that again.

It isn't any fun being a victim. It feels a lot better flexing your economic muscles against Big Oil.

So let's go for the jugular.

The time is right for our country to make a significant change in the way we consume energy. Because we are the center of the automotive industry, Michigan is in a key position to help the country make this transition.

In Lansing this summer, Michigan's Republicans and Democrats came together and passed key laws to promote our energy independence.

Henry Ford, who practically invented the auto industry, believed that ethanol, a form of alcohol distilled from agricultural products, was the logical fuel to power the car. Almost a century later, we just might fulfill his original vision.

There are several good reasons coming together at the same time to change from gas to biofuels like biodiesel and ethanol. We have been dependent on foreign source of oil for decades. But the downside of that dependence – the war in Iraq, our entanglement with unsavory regimes, and the uncertainty of the supply – is hard to ignore any longer. It is clear that greater energy independence would be a way to protect America's greatest value – our freedom.

It also makes good economic sense for us to develop our own energy resources. Rather than send our dollars overseas to purchase raw materials, we could employ our own people to produce energy here.

At a time when the economy is stagnant and unemployment is high, wouldn't it make sense to create a decentralized industry that gave farmers a new market for their products, that took advantage of waste and turned it into energy, and that created construction jobs to build plants to produce fuel? Wouldn't it make sense to create jobs operating those plants and distributing the fuel?

Isn't it better to pay our own people to create energy than to send the money overseas to buy oil from countries that hate us?

Usually we view respect for the environment and the needs of industry as exclusive and competing interests. But, this time, the two hold the promise of working together to solve one of our biggest problems.

Ethanol has some important environmental advantages over gasoline. It contains about 80% less environmental contaminants than gas, and it degrades quicker in water, so spills are not as harmful. With scientific evidence demonstrating the dangers of Global Warming, it is comforting to note that ethanol reduces greenhouse emissions, including carbon dioxide. An ethanol fuel known as E-85 also has lower hydrocarbon and benzene emissions than gas.

E-85 is a blend of 85% ethanol and 15% gasoline, and it can be burned in about 50 different vehicle models. The modifications to current vehicles are minimal. E-85 requires metal fuel tanks, bigger fuel injectors, and new software on Flexible Fuel Vehicles (FFVs) which could burn anything from 100% gasoline to E-85.

The good news is that Ford and GM are way ahead in the production of FFVs. They have 50 different vehicles that are FFVs and are geared to produce even more.

So there are good environmental, economic, foreign policy, and national defense reasons to develop alternative energy like ethanol. To top it off, ethanol is competitively priced, if not a bargain, for the consumer. The Amoco station in Rochester Hills was selling ethanol for $2.49 a gallon and regular unleaded for $2.79, the last time we checked. In Minnesota the differential is 40 to 50 cents a gallon. As we move forward to greater production of ethanol, economics of scale should permit us to produce it even cheaper. And the world price of oil seems headed for additional increases.

The Midwest is leading the way toward biofuels. Minnesota went from 11 gas stations selling 6,000 gallons of E-85 in 1998 to 200 stations pumping 7 million gallons in 2005. Iowa, the largest producer of ethanol in the U.S., just passed a law mandating renewable fuels usage of 10% in 2009 and increasing thereafter to 25%. Internationally, Brazil achieved near independence from oil by converting to ethanol made from sugar cane.

Michigan is moving toward ethanol. We already have stations selling E-85 in Dearborn Heights, Southfield, Rochester Hills, and Dimondale. Meijers recently announced that 20 stations around the state will begin selling E-85, including one in Warren, and new outlets by various retailers are coming to Detroit, Adrian, and Greenville. Ford is subsidizing the installation of ethanol pumps throughout the Midwest. Congress passed legislation to double national production of ethanol in the next five years, and I predict we will far surpass that.

In Michigan, we created a tax-free zone for a new $95 million ethanol plant in Marysville, and we have four other new plants under construction in Watervliet and Blissfield, and Barry and Calhoun Counties. We already have a 50-million-gallon-a-year plant operating in Caro.

We have reduced the tax on ethanol from 19 cents to 12 cents until they sell 2.5 billion gallons, and then the tax would revert to normal levels. That is a wise investment in a fledgling industry which will help it grow in viability. We also created ten new tax-free zones to encourage investments into renewable energy facilities. Finally, we mandated that state vehicle depots install E-85 and biodiesel fuel pumps and that the state steadily transform its own fleet into FFVs.

Alternative energy holds great promise for Michigan's economy. Biofuels are part of that equation, and they are an idea whose time has come.

September 2006

Life on a Rig: A Little Like Heaven, a Lot Like Prison

I spent the better part of a decade in Louisiana getting my education at LSU. But college was only half the education I got in Baton Rouge. I worked on an oil rig in the Gulf, and I also went fishing for crawfish in the Bayou. Those two experiences made a lasting impression on me. Sadly, the distinctive way of life I glimpsed is now threatened by the BP oil spill.

In the summer of 1981 I worked as a cook's helper on an oil rig in the Gulf of Mexico. It was minimum wage, but you got 12 hours a day 7 days a week, so 4 hours every day was at time and a half.

It was a lot like heaven and a lot like hell. Even with me doing the cooking, the food was great. So that part was like heaven. We're talking Jambalaya, Gumbo, Etouffee, and everything in unlimited quantities. As a starving student, I happily put on weight. The head cook learned his trade in the Army. As he described it, "The Army has the best food in the world. Until the cooks got hold of it!"

The rig was only accessible by a 2 hour helicopter ride, so in another way it was a lot like prison. Most people worked 7 days on and 7 days off, and beyond the kitchen, TV room, and bunkhouse, there was nowhere to go. So you were a prisoner in a confined space.

Out on the rig, all you could see in any direction was water. We worried about weather, especially hurricanes, but the likelihood of explosions or spills didn't seem realistic. In hindsight, we should have known better.

What has happened in the Gulf with the BP oil spill is a tragedy. It is a growing environmental disaster for all of us, but it is a particular disaster for the Cajun way of life I glimpsed one hot steamy day on the bayou. My New Orleans girlfriend and her father took me crawfishing, and it was one of the most enjoyable days of my life. You stick a bunch of little flat nets with an oversized safety pin and a bloody piece of meat on them in a shallow pond. Two crisscrossing loops of metal with a ribbon tied through them connect to the corners of the nets and sit about 3 inches above the water. Then you walk around with a long pole, lift up the net real fast, and every time there are 2 or 3 mudbugs, or crawfish, chawing on that bloody piece of meat.

In no time you have a bushel full of crawfish. But those days could be over if the marshes become fouled with oil and the fishing industry is destroyed. There does not seem to be an easy solution to the leak, and you begin to wonder how long it may continue and how bad the Gulf Coastline may be harmed. That may seem like an abstraction, but glimpsing the Cajuns and their way of life provides a personal sense of the enormity of this tragedy.

There are no easy answers. Louisiana, and the US economy both depend on oil. That is a reality. But a devastated ecosystem is also a reality. I learned to love the Cajun people of Louisiana and their rich culture. We have to learn a lesson and be a lot more careful before we make choices and take chances that could destroy a way of life.

May 2010

Budget Blues in Red

When You're in a Hole, Stop Digging

I knew it was gonna be a bad year back in January.

The economy had nose-dived and the Governor was in denial.

Out of his entire 43-page State of the State speech, the governor devoted exactly one-half of a page to the state's Budget Crisis.

He even got a little belligerent at one point. "I'll promise you one thing," he bellowed. "I won't leave a budget mess for my successor like my predecessor left me."

But the record tells a different story.

I am a fiscal conservative. And for the past four years I have agreed with my conservative colleagues that we must stay within our means. State spending has to be based on a stable funding source. We can not run a deficit.

Yet the Governor's final year in office finds us with a budget that does not reflect those sound principles. It is not sustainable. It is based on one-time revenue sources that will not be there next year.

The "rainy day fund" was at $1.2 billion. That will be zero by the end of this year. Debt is at an all-time high. The Medicaid trust fund has been drained of $400 out of its $500 million total, and that's before scheduled Medicaid reductions even begin. The state has a cash management problem and will have to borrow money next year just to pay its bills. The budget is awash in half a billion bucks of red ink. We are seriously out of balance with a structural deficit.

By any reasonable person's definition, that is a mess.

That's why I called a year and a half ago for Michigan to freeze both spending and taxes. The freeze would have saved $300 million last year and another $300 this year. The Macomb Daily agreed in an editorial, saying "We believe Switalski's proposal makes better sense than slashing the $11.5 billion school aid fund, where cuts could top the $300 million mark."

Somebody, somewhere has got to show some responsibility.

Meanwhile, despite the official Revenue Estimating Conference that revealed the State has a $430 million budget shortfall for Fiscal Year 2002, the legislature goes on its merry way, spending money and cutting taxes like there is no tomorrow. On the next legislative day after the deficit was revealed, the legislature went on with business as usual, granting a couple of tax breaks and spending money is doesn't have.

You'd think that $430 million in red ink might give a person pause.

But you'd be wrong.

It's hard to believe, but the House gave the Ryder Cup, the most popular and lucrative golf tournament in the world, a tax break. And that's not in order to lure them here—they'd already committed to Oakland Hills. The benefactors are large corporations who will now provide tax-free corporate hospitality packages.

The other wasn't much better. Legislators abolished a $1 application fee for a Sales Tax License that was set in 1932 and hadn't been raised since. That cost us a quick $150,000.

So while we're giving away money we need, we are spending money we don't have. The Capital Outlay budget funds building construction for state government and universities. We are only $80 million under our $2.7 billion bond cap, but the House voted to add additional projects and actually put us in the red by $210 million.

That's not what I call responsible.

Four years ago the state began a phase out of the single business tax. We cut it .1% each year for the next 24 years. The bill was introduced, passed committee, and passed the full House all in one day. That process usually takes several months. But when one party controls the House, the Senate, and the Governorship, they can make things happen instantly.

This flurry of activity all happened on June 2, 1999. I had only been in the House for 5 months. But even I knew something was wrong. People were criticizing the bill because you can't predict what the economy will do for 24 years. Should we still make the tax cut if we had a recession and the cut would create a deficit?

No.

Being good fiscal conservatives, legislators inserted a "trigger" into the bill. If the economy went sour and we blew our $1.2 billion "rainy day fund" down below $250 million, the trigger would engage and the tax cut would be suspended. Once the Rainy Day Fund got above $250 million, the annual tax cuts would resume.

I applauded my colleagues for adding the trigger, because I am very conservative fiscally. But I said the trigger was too low. I offered an amendment to raise it to $500 million. I argued that if we blew more than half our savings, we'd better take strong measures to stop the spiral and get our budget in order. If you waited until you'd spent the whole fund you'd be broke with no cushion left.

My amendment lost, 50-55, although I had some Republican support. Privately, some Republicans told me they agreed, but they were under pressure to pass the package in one day without any amendments.

That didn't make sense then, but what is happening in the legislature now makes even less sense.

Good fiscal conservatism was the basis for establishing a trigger. But now the Senate has passed a bill lowering the paltry $250 million trigger to . . . $1. That's not a typo. One dollar. Now I'm a Democrat, but I respect the Republican Party because it usually fights for fiscal responsibility.

Unfortunately, Republicans have abandoned their true principals of fiscal responsibility.

You get a better sense of the injustice of this when you consider the plight of the city of Eastpointe. Like most local units of government, Eastpointe funds many of its operations from state payments called Revenue Sharing. When the state took away the power of local governments to levy a sales tax, it guaranteed a certain portion of the state sales tax to the locals.

But the state has repeatedly cut these payments, and is proposing another $36 million cut as part of its latest reductions. Cities like Eastpointe, and Sterling Heights and Clinton Township now get less money from the state than they did in 2001. While costs have risen, these payments have gone down.

So Eastpointe has placed a 4 mill tax increase on the ballot. If voters don't approve it, they will have to start laying off police, firemen, and cutting city services.

In other words, Lansing legislators are cutting taxes, underfunding statutory revenue sharing payments, and forcing locals to raise their taxes. The taxpayer isn't going to see a tax cut if big business pays less in state taxes and he has to pay more in local taxes.

That's just a tax shift.

Some other shifts are even more troubling. Job One of government is to provide for public safety. Crime is down in large part because we have locked up criminals and kept them in jail so they can't get out and commit new crimes. What would a real conservative say if they knew the Governor and the legislature were closing prisons in order to balance the budget and save the tax cuts?

I don't know about you, but that's money I don't want to save. I don't want any criminal set free, let out early or paroled because we don't have room for them in the jails. I fear that our hard won reductions in crime are being sacrificed to these promised tax cuts.

Republicans promised voters two things that are now in conflict: tax cuts and fiscal responsibility. It was a mistake to make a 24-year promise that can only be kept by abandoning sound fiscal principles. These times call for political courage in telling the public the hard truth and not what you think they want to hear.

May 2002

The Fourth Circle of Budget Hell

Undeterred by its $1billion deficit, the Michigan House continued on its merry spending ways in September by authorizing additional capital outlay spending for state building projects. Since it has become clear that the current administration has no plan for eliminating the deficit and returning the state budget to fiscal stability, I have been voting no on additional spending items.

As I detailed last year ("A Billion Bucks in the Hole," *The Insider*, vol 6, no 6, November 2001) the state was resorting to all kinds of accounting tricks and one-time fixes to balance the budget. As I predicted, we never did earn $50 million by selling a piece of property, and the $1.2 Billion Rainy Day Fund has about 23 cents left in it. We've raided the Medicaid Trust Fund for $400 million out of the $500 million we'd set aside for future cuts in Federal Medicaid payments, so we'll have no easy way to make that up.

In short, we've done what no responsible manager would ever do. We've built a budget with a structural deficit. Instead of freezing or cutting the spending programs to match them with the revenues available, we've raised cigarette taxes and blown our savings to keep spending at a level we can't sustain.

We're in for a hard landing.

Thankfully, the legislature overwhelmingly rejected the Governor's veto of all revenue sharing dollars to local governments like cities and townships. That might have made the state's budget look better, but it would have forced your local government to either raise your millage or cut services like police and fire. That's what is called literally "passing the buck." Although I was in the middle of my annual family vacation in Vermont, I took relish in flying back for one day solely to override the veto.

What is sad is that Republicans, who I would normally give high marks for fiscal responsibility, have abandoned their conservative principles. Although they control the House, Senate, and Governorship, they lack the discipline to hold down spending, stabilize revenues, and bring the budget into balance. Instead of freezing taxes and spending, they continue to cut taxes and spend more.

That won't work.

With the Capital Outlay additions, we've hastened our entry into the fourth circle of Budget Hell.

First, we've blown all our Capital, or Building money for the next 3 years. We have a paltry $80 million available under the Bond Cap thru 2004, because we've already spent the money available for 2002, 2003, and 2004. So we won't be doing any projects for the next few years. I sure hope we don't need any emergency repairs.

Second, we've delayed scheduled maintenance on our stock of buildings and equipment. That means more frequent breakdowns of systems and future repairs will be more expensive.

Third, we've taken building projects that we were paying cash for and converted them to bond payments. That increases the cost because we now have to pay interest on the borrowed money. It's a double whammy. Instead of earning interest on our savings and cash, we are paying interest on our debt.

Finally, we are selling assets like buildings to private companies, and then renting them back from them, so that we are now paying more to house state government agencies with nothing to show for it in the end.

My solution? Freeze taxes and spending. Therein lies the beginning of balance.

September 2002

Where Have the Fiscal Conservatives Gone?

As the State of Michigan begins its 4th consecutive year of fiscal stress, the struggle has become tiresome. Why did Republicans, with majorities in the House and Senate, and with John Engler in the Governor's office, fail to master the fiscal crisis? Can we expect anything different now? Has budget policy changed under Democratic Governor Granholm?

Consider the basic facts. There were two chief ingredients to the State budget deficits. These deficits are the product of large tax cuts and an economic recession. The recession and poorly performing economy result in fewer business transactions, and thus less sales tax revenue. They also mean higher unemployment, less overtime and lower earnings for workers, and thus less income tax revenue. Cuts to the rate of the Single Business Tax (SBT) and the Income Tax mean even less revenue to the government.

Given this context, it's revealing to look back now and evaluate budget actions during the current downturn. How did the Michigan government react when things turned bad in 2001? A budget report by the non-partisan *Senate Fiscal Agency* provides some surprising answers.

Governor Engler proposed a Fiscal Year (FY) 2001 General Fund appropriation of $9.6 Billion. Despite signs of a slowing economy, the legislature added another $80 million of spending to the Governor's original request, hiking spending to $9.7 Billion. So the Republican majority not only maintained spending at the start of the recession, they actually *increased* it. When the economy stalled and revenues failed to come in as projected, the additional spending raised the FY 01 deficit from $648 million to $728 million.

That wasn't *fiscally responsible*. Nevertheless, Michigan's Constitution requires the budget to be balanced. So you might expect that the legislature returned to make budget cuts in Fall.

It didn't happen. Engler and the Republican House and Senate agreed upon a package of one-time revenue fixes to plug the budget holes. One-time fixes are so named because they only work for one year. If you spend all your savings to make your car payments *this* year, you can't use them to make your car payment *next year*. You've already spent them.

In like fashion, the Governor and legislature raided the Rainy Day Fund and the Tobacco Settlement Trust Fund for $290 million, and drained year end balances and work project accounts for another $250 million. By converting cash payments for state buildings to debt financing, they generated another $200 million. All in all, Engler and the Republican majority agreed to $755 million in one-time fixes.

In summary, fiscally responsible Republicans cut nothing, spent more, and created a $728 million structural imbalance in the state budget. A structural imbalance means that on a continuing basis, you are pledged to spend more than you can support in revenues. If you wanted to fund state government at *exactly the same level* the following year, with no increases, you'd be starting off $728 million in the hole.

Reality was actually worse. Because of the recession, Michigan started FY 2002 with *even less money* than we had in 2001. Plus we had to make up $728 million in one-time fixes.

Compounding the problem, Governor Engler was slow to adjust to the new fiscal reality. His proposed FY 02 budget was $9.8 Billion, an *increase* of $200 million from his FY 01 budget. And he and the legislature had made no fundamental reductions to the budget. At the same time, he remained committed to *cutting* revenues through his twin tax cuts, despite an economic recession that was rapidly *shrinking* general revenues.

General Fund revenues dropped so significantly that the FY 02 deficit reached $1.5 Billion, more than doubling the $728 Million shortfall of the year before. *This* time the legislature acted by cutting spending proposed by the Governor. But the cuts fell far short of what was necessary to bring about a structural balance. The legislature trimmed $663 million from the Governor's proposal, and again drew on one time revenue sources to maintain the rest of the budget. The legislature tapped the Rainy Day Fund for another $450 million and used various other transfers and shifts from the Tobacco and Merit Award Trust Funds to find $960 million in one time revenue.

This represents a second year of stop gap measures adopted by Republicans to escape the budget mess without making the fundamental reforms necessary to address the structural imbalance.

Finally, in FY 03, Engler actually proposed a budget lower than the previous year's. The FY 03 General Fund proposal came in at $9.3 Billion. That was $500 million less than his FY 02 proposal. But that proposal itself had been $1.5 Billion out of balance, and revenues would fall again to make this new budget $1.4 Billion short.

The legislature cut the Governor's proposal an additional $478 million further, leaving another $1 billion to be made up by - you guessed it - one-time revenue fixes. But for the first time, the legislature actually raised revenue by increasing the cigarette tax. Combined with a pause in the SBT tax rollback, the two measures produced $200 million in new revenue.

Hindsight is 20-20, but this review demonstrates that even Republican legislators, with a reputation for fiscal conservatism and control of the House, Senate, and Governor's office, failed to make the tough choices necessary to balance the state's budget on a continuing basis.

They failed on two sides of the budget equation. First, Republicans avoided making budget cuts sufficient to achieve balance, and instead relied heavily on one-time cuts.

Second, they didn't stabilize revenues. Why not admit the annual tax cuts, adopted in the go-go years of the late 90s, were unsustainable during a recession? The cuts should have been paused until the economy recovered. Instead Republicans clung to tax cuts adopted when state revenues were increasing by almost 7% per year.

But times were now very different. In fact, revenues dropped from a projected $9.6 Billion in FY 01 to an anemic $7.8 billion in FY 03.

So what if Republicans failed to live up to their reputation for Fiscal Responsibility? Have Democrats done any better? When Governor Granholm took over in January of 2003, how did she close the billion dollar gap she inherited?

The Governor's first budget was her FY 04 proposal. As the table demonstrates, Governor Engler consistently overestimated available revenue when he proposed his budgets during the downturn. Governor Granholm made this same mistake, proposing $8.6 Billion in spending for FY 04 when revenues came in at only $7.8 billion. She cut deeper than Engler, trimming $700 million from the previous budget. But she acquiesced in a

$200 million increase added by the legislature. That resulted in a $1 Billion deficit.

General Fund Budget *(in billions)*					
	FY00	FY01	FY02	FY03	FY04
Governor's Budget	9.1	9.6	9.8	9.3	8.6
Final Appropriation	9.6	9.7	9.1	8.8	8.8
Revenue	9.8	9.0	8.3	7.9	7.8
Surplus/Deficit	+.2	-.7	-.8	-.9	-1.0

Why the systemic optimism?

There are three reasons. All Governors' Budget proposals are political documents. They are the opening phase in negotiations with the legislature. Budget Proposals generally spend what the experts say is available to spend. But the State Treasurer, the Governor's appointee, is one of the experts, and overestimating your budget by $1 Billion is usually not good tactics.

Secondly, it's also true that 4 straight years of declining revenue are unprecedented in Michigan, and economists can be forgiven for expecting a quicker turnaround based on past experience. But fool me once, shame on you. Fool me twice, shame on me.

Finally, a significant part of the deficits has been the tax cuts. It shouldn't be so surprising that revenues would fall when we continue to cut tax rates each year. Economists at the Revenue Conference in January pointed out that more than half of the $500 Billion Federal Deficit is directly attributable to the Bush tax cuts. Michigan's deficit is no different. It's called doing the same thing over and over and expecting different results.

Granholm will be proposing her second budget soon. Will it break the cycle of proposing a spending level significantly higher than ultimate revenues? If it doesn't, we will continue to face mid year cuts that cause havoc to efficient operations. A responsible proposal would strike a balance by cutting spending again, while raising enough revenue to provide a cushion if the economy continues to sputter.

February 2004

Is Now the Time to Cap State Revenues

Candy, pop, and no school. Another helping of dessert and one more beer.

Sometimes the things that seem good aren't really good for you. In the case above, you can end up dumb, with rotten teeth, a big belly and a hangover.

During the recent jousting over Governor Granholm's proposal to help the Automotive Sector by cutting taxes on manufacturers, the Michigan Senate responded by passing a series of bills that would put a cap on State Revenues. This would make our state's financial picture much worse, but also would affect the quality of services that Michigan's residents expect from their state and local governments. It would result in more cuts to education and local governments.

The initiative would limit the growth of tax revenue and state spending to the rate of inflation plus one percent, with the first $50 million in excess going toward further business tax credits and anything after that being split between additional business tax cuts and the state's rainy-day fund.

At first hearing, that might sound good. Some compromise is necessary to help our manufacturers. But I believe both sides can agree on how to reform business taxes without adding this Cap idea. This additional proposal to cap revenues would place our state's schools, our state's safety, and our state's social net in grave danger in the process.

Michigan has long ridden the cycle of economic boom and bust. Our hope for recovery is what gets us through the tough times. Where is Michigan in the crest and trough cycle? We are in a trough. The non-partisan Senate Fiscal Agency will attest to the fact that we are in the bottom of the trough. Is this the time to set a cap on state revenues?

Oh, I'm sorry. There already is a cap on state revenues. It's in our Constitution and we are $5 billion below that cap. We are indeed at a historic trough in terms of state revenue.

Is this the time to set a cap on state revenue?

I'm glad you asked that question because a similar proposal was reviewed in July by the Senate Appropriations Committee. I must report, in all honesty, that it got a very cool reception. In fact, Shirley Johnson, the Chair of Appropriations and a Republican with 25 years of experience in the Legislature, was particularly eloquent in her analysis of the shortcomings of a cap, that takes as its baseline, a historic trough.

What is the vision behind this proposal? It is an empty vision. It is a vision that says now that we have starved state revenue into cardiac arrest; let's drag it into the bathroom and choke it to death. That is not a positive vision for the State of Michigan. When we had money, we used to run an efficient state government. We paid for capital improvements through self-financing when it made sense. Now we sell our buildings, lease the space back, and pay a premium for the privilege. We used to earn on our rainy-day fund. Now we pay interest on money we borrowed to make ends almost meet. We securitize our tobacco settlement and mortgage tomorrow.

What would suggest that now is the appropriate time to limit state revenues?

We've emptied state government of its rainy-day fund. We've emptied local governments of their fund balances. We've emptied school districts of their unencumbered reserves, and we have emptied revenue sharing to a historic low, such that nearly one thousand of the state's 1,242 townships now get no, zero statutory revenue sharing. We have emptied revenue sharing to the point where none, zero of Michigan's 83 counties have gotten a revenue sharing appropriation in the last two years, and we have an increasing number of cities in receivership. We have gone from a dream of full funding of revenue sharing to a nightmare of empty funding of revenue sharing. That is the vision of this proposal.

What about education? The state now provides 16 percent of the University of Michigan's funding. The state contribution to universities now averages about a third of the cost of an education. Community colleges don't even get that. They have historically relied on a three-legged stool for funding, combining state appropriation, local millage, and tuition. The stool is now two-legs straddling a tightrope. Is this the vision that will prepare Michigan to compete in the new economy?

Apologists for this plan assert that it won't affect K-12 education. That is as true as saying that the Lottery will fix the funding problems for schools. Yes, it is true that the lottery fund goes to schools. But it is also true that the state reduced its General Fund contribution dollar-for-dollar to the School Aid Fund.

So yes, it is true that the single business tax cuts affect the General Fund and not the School Aid Fund. That ignores the larger truth that the General Fund used to contribute over $400 million to the School Aid Fund. That contribution is down to virtually zero now because the General Fund is perpetually broke. We have never replaced the $400 million we cut. In fact, we keep shifting new responsibilities from the General Fund to the School Aid Fund, increasing the burden on the School Aid Fund. Passing this plan will mean the School Aid Fund will never recover to its median level. Is this a vision for Michigan's future?

It is not my vision.

December 2005

Cut More?

Many of my e-mail correspondents suggest the state can fix its budget problems like any business or family does. The state, my e-advisors say, should just cut more.

The suggestion is appealing in its simplicity, but everyone underestimates just how hard it is to cut when you have to get 56 House members, 20 Senators, and a Governor to agree on the cuts. And these officials will only cut if they think the public supports the cuts.

When my advisors suggest running the state like a business, I hope they don't mean Enron. And though it would be nice to get a $400 million retirement bonus, I hope they don't mean Exxon-Mobil either.

When they suggest running the state like any family does, do you want to be in a family that tells their kids to drop out of school and get a job to help pay the bills? Or sells their house in today's market and moves in with mom? Or is forced to declare bankruptcy and move to another state?

I hope these advisors just mean that we should put some money in the bank, that we should balance expenditures with revenues, and treat everyone as our brothers and sisters.

I agree with that.

But that is different from just cut more.

So let's analyze what Just Cut More actually means.

First, no matter how much you cut, it is never enough. So this advice will never go out of date, because you can always cut more until there is nothing left. In the abstract, it always seems possible to cut more.

As a corollary, no matter what you cut, you will not gain acceptance or recognition of the cuts, because just cut more always implies that you didn't cut enough.

Secondly, when you do cut, just cut more advocates will complain that you should have cut something else. Just cut more is vague, but when you talk about specific cuts, or program elimination, people will object that they didn't mean to cut that.

People write to me often saying, cut more, but don't cut education, because education is our future. So cut someone else. I don't know anyone who advocates cutting veterans, especially when so many are dying in Iraq. People object when we cut police or fire, because you can't cut public safety because that is Job Number One of government. Local officials got together recently to protest cuts to local government. When the Macomb Daily asked them how the state should resolve its budget problems, they suggested the state should cut more. But don't cut local government grants.

You get the idea.

The way government usually cuts is by starving programs. People will object more to the elimination of a program than to freezing its funding. So if you want to succeed, you seek the path of least resistance. If you are trying to make a change, people will fight you less, so government tends to work through measured, incremental changes. That's a good thing, because it puts an emphasis on stability and manages the disruptions of change.

The budget deal that was hammered out last week has been criticized because it used lots of accounting gimmicks and borrowing and pushed spending into next year, rather than making the tough cuts or raising needed revenues. In truth, that has been the approach for 6 years now, but the approach is wearing thin.

So what would $1 billion in cuts actually look like?

A conservative think tank proposed privatizing all of the state's 15 universities. Basically, that means the state should no longer subsidize the cost of college for kids. Now I know tuition is high, but compare the average annual tuition at the state's private institutions of $18,000 a year with the average tuition of $7,400 at the state's 15 public institutions. When we just cut more, should we more than double the tuition cost for you and your kids? Is that the best way to make Michigan competitive in the new economy?

Nevertheless, we did cut more, another $25 million from Community Colleges and $166 million from Universities. That is a deep cut, so expect tuition bills to rise next year.

So the state cut Higher Education deeply again.

But guess what?

It's not enough. Just cut more.

What about state employees?

In September, 2001, after nearly 3 years of total Republican control in Lansing under Governor Engler, with Republican majorities in the House and Senate, the State Government workforce stood at 62,000. I say this not for partisan purposes, but to suggest that 62,000 was a reasonable number of employees. You would think that with 3 years of total Republican control that the number of employees was not inflated, and that it was what was absolutely necessary to get the job of state government done. Today, the workforce is 52,000, a cut of over 10,000 employees, a reduction of 17%.

In 1996, there were 250,000 welfare cases. As of today, there are 78,000, a decrease of 300%. And this despite bad economic times when hard working people have lost their jobs, exhausted their unemployment, declared bankruptcy, and gone on welfare. Spending on welfare in 1996 was about $900 million. Half of that was state money, the other half was federal. Welfare consumed 4% of the state budget. Today, we spend $400 million, half of that being state money, and it amounts to 2% of our budget today. Total spending on welfare has decreased by 50%, despite our awful economy.

But guess what?

It's not enough. Cut more.

I could make a lot of criticisms of the budget deal, but I won't. I was part of the discussions, and it was the best we could do and still get a majority vote in each chamber. Everyone else who had a supposedly better idea, just couldn't seem to get a sufficient number of colleagues to agree with them. Maybe that's because those ideas weren't so good after all.

June 2007

Broken Promise:
Why We Must Cut College Scholarships

Michigan's Promise Scholarship was created in 2000 (as the Michigan Merit Award) during a great economy by then Governor John Engler. The revenue source was annual payments from Tobacco Settlement dollars, and the cost was about $60 million. The state was having difficulty getting students to take the MEAP test, and schools had to bribe students with days off, free pizza, and other inducements to get them to stop boycotting the test.

The $2,500 scholarship motivated students, and participation zoomed. The scholarship was available to all students, regardless of income. They just had to pass the test. Critics complained that the Tobacco money should have been devoted to health-related programs, and that the money was going to students who had no financial need and who might already be on full scholarship. But I voted for it, because I thought there ought to be at least one scholarship based purely on merit, to reward good students, and the state had a lot of money at the time.

Good times don't last forever, and within two years the state began having terrible budget problems. The history of the Promise Scholarships shows that the legislature has repeatedly changed the rules on the amount and timing of the grants, driven by a need to cut spending. Unfortunately, to make the cuts palatable, the state has raised spending for future years. As a result, the program has escalated from an $82 million annual commitment to nearly $200 million.

The first change came in 2003. The cost had grown to $121 million in 2002, as more and more students were taking and retaking the test until they qualified. In 2003, the scholarship was changed from $2,500 upon graduating from High School to $1,250 the first year and $1,250 the second year. The change appeared innocuous, since students got the same $2,500 total, but it saved the state $60 million.

Just think of it. The first year, your cost is cut in half, because you only have to pay $1,250 instead of $2,500 to 50,000 high school seniors. But the savings are short lived. The second year, you have to pay the new seniors their $1,250, plus last year's seniors the second half of their payment. Bingo, you are back to $132 million.

Other changes followed, such as restricting scholarships to in-state students. In 2007 we changed the two $1,250 payments into two $1,000 payments at the end of the freshman and sophomore year of college followed by a $2,000 payment after the completion of an Associate's degree.

Once again this saved money up front, about $24 million, but at a significant increase in future costs.

Official estimates show the cost escalating annually to $192 million in 2015. Unfortunately, this is typical of government. Faced with making a cut to a popular program, politicians promise future improvements in return for short-term savings. The improvements are never paid for. So immediate budget relief leads to a growing unfunded liability.

Don't get me wrong. Scholarships are a nice thing. Especially when you can pay for them. But tobacco settlement dollars have dwindled. Besides, when you are cutting everything in state government, shouldn't Scholarships have to take their share of the pain? 10 years ago, this program didn't even exist.

How can it now be so crucial that it shouldn't even face a reduction?

Many argue that it is a promise made to students. But the history we have just described shows that promise has been altered many times. The promise was made in good faith, but economic reality and recession have made it impossible to keep that promise.

I recently served on a panel interviewing students for the Winning Futures scholarship program. This organization works with High School students to get them to plan their future, form a career goal, and develop the specific steps they must take to make their goal a reality. I will never forget the young lady who told the panel she had planned to go to University, but that she had to change her plan, because both of her parents had lost their jobs. She began to cry and said that she had gotten a job to help her family and that she would have to go to Community College.

I reassured her that her parents should be proud to have such a fine daughter. Imagine another child, selfish enough to insist that her parents lose their house, sell their possessions, and do whatever they had to do to keep their promise to pay her college tuition. I would submit that such a daughter is not worth educating. Which daughter would you rather have?

The supposed ideal of a free college education does not stand scrutiny anyway. I have always believed that the best thing my late father ever did for me was to not pay for my education. He gave me a job in his tombstone shop, making grave markers to earn enough money to pay for my own education. I valued it more because I paid for it. Every year when I finished classes, I was sick of school. Then came a 3 month dose of reality. After a summer of wrestling with granite blocks in the hot and dusty shop, I couldn't wait to get back to school.

That's just human nature. If education, or health care, or ice cream is free, we don't properly value it. We waste it. We abuse it. But if we have to pay, even part of the cost, we start using it carefully, because our own money is at stake.

My conclusion, which many of my own colleagues disagree with, is that the Promise Scholarship should take its fair share of the cuts, just like everything else. Some think that is bad politics, because the program is very popular. But it is the right policy in our present circumstances.

September 2009

Politics

House Fails to Ban Tongue Splitting

This just in from the Insane Asylum in Lansing. An attempt to ban Tongue Splitting in Michigan failed recently when the House fell two votes short of passing House Bill 4688.

I am not making this up.

Tongue Splitting, according to the official staff analysis, "is a form of body modification that involves cutting the tongue, generally down the middle, separating the tongue into left and right halves, and preventing the halves from growing back together." This can be achieved with a laser, scalpel, or even fishing wire. The result is a "forked" tongue like a serpent's. Tongue Splitting has "become something of a fad in certain circles in California."

Why am I not surprised?

Now I know the Michigan Legislature has a lot of important business to take care of, like a $1 billion budget deficit. And I don't think there is a rash of people filling the tattoo and body piercing parlors, demanding to have their tongues split. But that's what I love about Lansing. Any representative can introduce a bill and if the leadership decides to take it up, you must vote on it.

Even if it's absurd.

The debate centered on two points. Opponents of the bill claimed that government should stay out of people's mouths. If people want to do this, let them do it. There is no reason for the state to get involved in every lunatic idea that anyone comes up with.

Advocates of the ban argued that not only is the idea crazy, but the procedure often leads to serious infection and even death.

In the end, the bill was defeated by a strange coalition of the extreme liberals, who believe that people ought to be able to do whatever they want, and the ultra-conservatives, who believe that government shouldn't regulate anything.

I voted to ban tongue splitting. I figure that anyone who splits their tongue doesn't have health insurance. And if they have insurance, I'll bet if you check the rider, it doesn't cover complications arising from a botched tongue splitting.

When that person shows up in the emergency room for treatment, and has no money or insurance, by law the hospital has to treat them. That cost is ultimately borne by taxpayers. That's you and me.

And this tongue says it doesn't want to subsidize those tongues.

June 2002

A Holiday Prayer

Under the Rules of the Senate, each member, on a rotating basis, is called upon to give the Invocation, or prayer, at the start of the daily session. By change, my turn came on the day after the November 2008 Election. I felt privileged to have the opportunity to offer a prayer on this important day.

A vote in the Senate is called a "division." But in democracy, a division yields a decision. And after the decision, responsible people stop fighting and arguing and hopefully work together to implement the decision fairly.

It was in this spirit I offered the following prayer.

"Good morning, Lord. Once again, Lord, You have made all things new. Since the sun set yesterday, the whole world has changed. Things that we though we knew, we now know are not so. Excuse us, Lord, while we take a moment to start in wonder at this new day that You have made.

We made a big decision last night. We chose new leaders. But I hear Your inspiration in the words of one of the people we did not choose. My friend, John McCain, who You know I have voted for twice, gave a magnificent concession speech last night, gracious in defeat, with an appreciation for the historic moment, and with a pledge to support our new President in finding was to bridge our differences and find solutions to our problems.

Lord, many of us who voted for President Obama love John McCain. Let him know that we respect the work he has done. Just because we didn't vote for him is not a rejection. I think from his words last night, he already knows that. Lord, help him show us what it means to be a loyal opposition.

Today is a day of redemption. Americans have been prisoners for centuries on an evil legacy. Slavery made prisoners of both master and slave. Today that power seems irreversibly broken, and that sin has been washed away. Today all men and women are brothers and sisters. We have lived up to our ideals that we are all God's children, equal in Your eyes. We have chosen according to individual merits and not race or skin color. We have been liberated.

We still have great problems to solve, Lord. As President-elect Obama said, the decision we made last night is not in itself the change we seek. But it creates the opportunity, the possibility that we can fix our problems. We need Your help and inspiration, and we need to work together to do that. Lord, help us to do that. Amen."

I believe my prayer has been heard. The good Lord has inspired Mr. Obama to meet with two of his chief campaign rivals, Senator McCain and Senator Clinton. They talked and worked on common interests. Such meetings between winner and loser are unprecedented. But they reflect exactly the magnanimous spirit I petitioned for with my prayer.

November 2008

Straight Talk on Prisons

My cousin Johnny has a son, Jon Switalski, who just ran for County Commissioner in Warren. Jon is a fine young man who worked on Congressman Bonior's staff. He has helped me campaign a lot over the years, and is generally a credit to the family and his community. But politics can be a nasty game, and Jon was the victim of 6 glossy, mudslinging campaign mailings. Several attacked him for votes I had cast in the Senate, and another dressed him up as a hippie, and all of them just plain lied about him.

This literature was condemned by the *Detroit News*, the *Detroit Free Press*, and the *Macomb Daily* as unfair, scurrilous, untrue, shameless, and demagoguery. Jon vigorously refuted the charges, but I am proud to say he never descended to the negative level of his opponent. And he continued to work hard throughout the campaign, knocking on doors every afternoon and dropping literature every morning.

To their credit, the voters of Warren rejected the negative campaigning and rewarded Jon with a resounding 60%-40% win.

So I devoted my last Insider to correcting the distortions the mudslingers made of my record, and hand delivered it in Northwest Warren. I'll repeat some of what I said there, because I think these campaign attacks are revealing.

They've been the stock in trade of the mudslinging garbage that has marred Warren politics for years.

One of the slick attack pieces suggested, in words and bogus pictures, that Michigan's prisons are posh exercise clubs, where beautiful women in fancy leotards relax and jazzercize. It charged that the "Switalskis" want to raise your taxes and spend the money on prisoner education and quality of life programs.

As the ranking Democrat on the Senate Appropriations Committee for Corrections, I have visited several of Michigan's prisons.

You wouldn't want to be there.

I didn't want to be there, but I felt it was part of my job to review operations. The huge cellblock at Jackson looks exactly like what you see in The Shawshank Redemption. We run a better prison than they did, but it's still no place anyone would ever want to be.

Is prison a picnic?

Macomb County Sheriff Mark Hackel taught me long ago that you control prisoners with rewards and punishments. TV and work detail outside the jail are privileges that prisons strive for, and if they misbehave you take those rewards away, until they correct their behavior.

So let's talk about prison education.

Among the few positive opportunities for prisoners in Michigan's jails are the Vocational Education programs. The Michigan Department of Corrections swears by them. Isn't it smarter to teach prisoners a trade so they can get a legitimate job when they get out of prison? So they can pay taxes like you and I do? Or do we want to release convicts after they've served their time, knowing only how to commit more crimes? Do we want a revolving door back to prison so we can spend $30,000 a year housing and guarding perpetual prisoners?

Studies from other states indicate a 25% reduction in recidivism for prisoners who left prison after completing vocational training. With Michigan's prisons bursting at the seams, and state revenue down, doesn't it make sense to do something to keep people from committing new crimes and reentering prison?

My colleagues in the Senate think so. We voted 37-0 for the Corrections Budget, which funds prisoner education. All 22 Senate Republications joined 15 Democrats and voted for House

Bill 4390. So there is unanimous bi-partisan agreement that these educational programs make sense.

I also helped establish another effort. I brought the Director of the Department of Corrections together in my office with officials from the University of Michigan. Several professors at U of M wanted to volunteer their time to teach a class for Women Prisoners. The women get no credit for it, but if they get out of prison and start going to college, they can petition the university for advance placement credit. This program cost the state and the taxpayer nothing, but about 40 women prisoners are participating in it. The women prisoners work hard in the class, and even asked that the class be made harder.

How many teachers anywhere have ever had that request?

The teachers volunteer because they feel the university should contribute to a better society, and also because they find it so gratifying to teach women who are so desperate for redemption and a glimmer of hope for a better life.

That is the reality behind prisoner education.

It is the hope that at least a few prisoners can correct themselves and change their lives. Although you wouldn't know it from reading this article, we had to cut the vocational education budget for prisons this year. Times are tough and we just don't have enough money to even maintain last year's efforts. It's a cut I made reluctantly, but it had to be made.

As a taxpayer, I hope that you would understand and accept that.

Instead, the campaign trash seeks to corrupt you. It appeals to your basest instincts. Rather than educate you, it attempts to deceive you. Instead of using politics to uplift people, this shameless literature advances the absurd suggestion that prisoners have it better than you. It seeks to stir up your hatred against criminals by making you jealous of them.

You deserve better than that.

We should expect our leaders to inspire us, to call upon us to do great things, and make our city or county, state or country the best it can be. That's how leaders should earn our respect.

Now consider this. Who has done more to inform you of the reality behind Michigan's prisons? People who tell you with fake glossy pictures that they are fancy exercise clubs, or the

Switalskis, who have successfully prosecuted scores of criminals, sentenced them to prison, and are currently spending $2.1 billion a year to keep them locked up and away from you?

Which behavior are you going to reward with your vote?

The voters of Warren rejected the campaign trash and voted overwhelmingly for Jon Switalski.

I think they made the right choice.

November 2004

Bailout: The Art of the Deal

How did Congress approve a $700 billion Wall Street Bailout, when the proposal was roundly criticized by both opponents and supporters, and opposed by some 84% of the electorate? How could such a universally hated plan pass Congress so quickly, just 30 days before a National Election?

This is a fascinating question that provides a peek into the inner workings of our democracy. But no one ever explains how such things actually happen. If you read this story, I will tell you how.

Here's the classic legislative problem: How do you pass a law *that must pass*, but that everyone hates and no one wants to vote for?

Already many readers are leaping to their feet with outraged objections! Why must the bill pass, they ask? If the law is terrible, and everyone hates it, should it not be defeated?

No.

Because our Leadership decided *it had to pass.*

While we may disagree, our National Leaders concluded that the Bailout was necessary. President Bush proposed it, the Democratic Speaker of the House and Senate Majority Leader supported it, as did the Republican House and Senate Minority Leaders. The Treasury Secretary and Chair of the Federal Reserve, the supposed experts, supported it. And both of the Presidential candidates supported it.

They all came to the conclusion that *it had to pass.*

You may disagree, but that was their conclusion.

Now how did they get it done?

The Bailout represents the Supreme Legislative Challenge. Again: *How do you pass a law that everyone hates and no one wants to vote for?*

I will tell you, because I have been in this situation many times. As recently as last Fall, I was the sponsor of a bill establishing a Medicare Estate Recovery Program. Everyone in Lansing hated the bill. Michigan was the only state not complying with Federal Requirements to have such a program. We had refused to comply for 14 years. But now the Feds were threatening, in writing, to fine us hundreds of millions of dollars. So my bill, that everyone hated, had to pass.

It passed.

Here is how such things are done. And while I was not there, I am sure this is how the Bailout was done.

First, leadership on both sides of the aisle, and in both the House and Senate chambers, agrees face to face that the bill has to pass. And they agree to work together to get the necessary votes. Say you are the Republican and I am the Democrat. Say there are 100 members in our chambers, so we need 51 votes. I say to you, I will get 25 of my guys, and you get 25 of yours. Together with our own votes, we will have 52 and the bill will pass.

You might say you only have 40 members and I have 60. You suggest we each get half of our respective delegations, meaning you 20 and me 30. There are many variations on the deal, but in essence, we are agreeing to jointly engineer passage with roughly equal contributions from both sides. The bi-partisan nature of the deal is essential, because neither side can effectively use the issue against the other party if most of their own members voted for it.

This is especially important when the public thinks it hates the bill.

Like most things that are effective, the deal is surprisingly simple. When votes are lopsided, it is because one side wants it more than the other, or for a variety of other reasons. Clearly this was the type of deal behind the Bailout.

And that's the easy part. The hard part is getting the votes.

As you rise higher in government, the members get more sophisticated. Many won't tell you how they are going to vote. So when you are trying to count votes, you get a lot of "I will probably vote for it," or "I am leaning against it." Some members want to tie resolution of other issues to their vote. The process can be like swimming in a pool of sharks.

When the House put it up for a vote, two-thirds of the Democrats voted yes, and only one third of Republicans and it failed by a dozen votes. Speaker Nancy Pelosi was criticized for the failure, but the deal had broken down. The whole world was watching, so the vote couldn't be delayed. But Pelosi couldn't allow what was supposed to be a bi-partisan bill pass with only a third of Republicans supporting it.

General George Patton once said, "You don't win a war by dying for your country. You win by making the other guy die for his country." If you are trying to win a partisan war, you win by making the other guy vote for, and pass, the hated bill. And you need it to pass, because otherwise you are subject to blame for its failure, and any bad consequences that flow from that failure.

Politics is a strange world, isn't it?

When you are trying to get bi-partisan cooperation, you normally don't make a fiery partisan speech right before the vote. But when the President and Congressional Leaders of your own party ask for your vote, two-thirds of you don't normally say no either.

The defeat surprised everyone. Republican Minority Leader Mitch McConnell was quoted as saying the Senate had to take up the bill immediately after House passage, rather than allow time for opposition to organize in the Senate. Both he and the Democratic leaders wanted bi-partisan cooperation. But then the House failed to pass the bill. Most significantly, the Stock Market dropped 777 points upon news of the failure, and the magnitude of the crisis became clear to all.

The Senate took the lead and passed the bill with overwhelming bi-partisan support, 74-25. Many "sweeteners" were added to the bill, which have been condemned as "pork" but included such things as rolling back the alternative minimum tax on the middle class and extending tax credits for people who make their homes more energy efficient.

I don't think it is fair to characterize those items as pork. But I am sure the sharks found some flesh here and there.

The economic crisis is not over, and additional Federal actions may be necessary. Some of those actions may be unpopular. But what people really want is for the crisis to be averted. The best chance for that is if the Congress works together like they did on the Bailout. If the Bailout fails to end the crisis, Congress should work together to find another solution.

November 2008

Fiddling While Rome Burns

The number one issue facing Michigan today is jobs. We are struggling through a tough economy, and people are hurting. We should be redoubling our efforts to create economic opportunity for our citizens, but many of my colleagues in the Michigan Legislature have different ideas about what is important.

Instead of focusing on jobs, my conservative colleagues concentrated on some social issues as their last accomplishments before the November elections. I must confess to having different priorities.

Three actions struck me as particularly misguided.

First, the Chairmen of both the House and the Senate Education Committees prevailed upon the State Board of Education to delay new Science Requirements for High School Graduation. The delay was granted so that conservative legislators can add "Intelligent Design" or "Creationism" to the teaching of Evolution.

I do not believe that politicians or religious leaders should determine what is taught in our Science Classes. We lack the expertise. We should not be teaching religion under the guise of Science. But the Board of Education bent to the wishes of the conservative chairmen, who believe their particular vision of God should be enshrined in the curriculum.

Secondly, the House passed HB 5633, to establish English as Michigan's Official Language, and a Senate Committee recommended it for passage by the full Senate. Thanks to the integrity of the Senate Majority Leader, we did not take the bill up before the election.

The bill is an empty gesture. English is the language of Michigan because 99 and 44 one-hundredths percent of Michiganders speak only English, not because the legislature passes some bill. The bill says that no one can be compelled to translate English into any other language, except where required to by law. We only found one Michigan Law that requires the government to publish information in another language, and that was to inform pregnant women of the dangers of abortion. I am sure conservatives would not want to revoke that law, so making English the official language would have zero practical effect.

The bill is politically popular because it gives people a vague feeling that we are being tough on immigrants. But these same immigrants want to learn English. They beg us every year to fund English Language classes so they can learn to speak English and get a better job. If we really want to be tough on them, we should continue to cut the minimal funding we provide for these classes. Does that seem like a good way to ensure that people are more productive and stay off public assistance?

Finally, House Conservatives recycled an oldie—Drug Testing for Welfare Recipients. They passed HB 6481 almost two years to the date after they passed the same bill last time. By coincidence that also was just before the November elections. Once again the Senate Majority Leader did not take the bill up, and it will likely die a quiet death in December. But the issue is politically popular, and gathered media attention for a few days, and will likely appear in campaign literature. But just like its two predecessors in 2004 and 1999, it can never take effect because it is an unconstitutional violation of the 4th Amendment rules on illegal searches. The Federal Courts have already ruled so.

I will miss the Senate Majority Leader Ken Sikkema when he is gone. He is on the other side of the aisle and is very conservative, but he has great integrity. Unfortunately he is term limited out in December.

I hope the next person to hold the fiddle concentrates on jobs and not scoring cheap political points.

September 2006

Free Gonzo!

Roseville artist Edward "Gonzo" Stross is my neighbor. His famous mural is across the street from my District Office at Utica and Gratiot in the historic Roseville Theatre Building. I can look out my window every day and see his painting. Personally, I like it. Every few years he makes significant changes to it, and he frequently adds new elements. It's almost like a community bulletin board.

Many people in the area also enjoy seeing his work, because everyone can have an opinion about art, and the mural gives us a shared experience to gossip about, argue over, and pontificate about without coming to blows. I think that is a great thing. That wall interests and engages us. Gonzo's art provides one of the few occasions for a good argument with your friends, while still remaining friends.

That is priceless.

Gonzo has had a long running feud with the Roseville City Council. I have largely stayed out of these disputes. I have my own battles to fight in State Government, and I follow the principle that you should stay out of other people's disputes unless you are affected or have a very good reason. The Council doesn't need me to tell them how to run their business. I might express my opinion, privately, if asked. But it's not wise to put your nose into everyone's business.

I would have stayed out of the dispute, but then Gonzo got sentenced to jail. At that point, I asked the ACLU to step in and take the case because I do not believe the government should have the power to put Gonzo in jail for painting his mural. Ex-prosecutor Carl Marlinga is now on the case.

Whether the government should have the power to deprive Gonzo of his liberty for painting that mural is an important question that deserves strict scrutiny. I think the fundamental question is whether the government has the right to regulate decorative painting on a citizen's private property. The City has argued that this mural is a sign, and therefore subject to the City's sign ordinance. I believe that ordinance is justified for advertising, but not for a decorative mural.

There's probably a limit to decoration. Even if it is your private property, you shouldn't be able to paint just anything on it. But by what right can the government say you can't paint LOVE or a copy of Michelangelo's Sistine Chapel?

I sympathize with the judge. Gonzo is sometimes his own worst enemy. When he said he wouldn't change his painting and no one could make him, the judge didn't have much choice. I just don't think it ever should have got that far.

The whole episode puts Roseville in a bad light. I hope that a more constructive solution can be found to the dispute. When Gonzo got in trouble for painting some graffiti on an abandoned property, he was sentenced to painting a beautiful mural of the Statue of Liberty on the VFW on Gratiot.

That was constructive. Sacred Heart is talking about having him paint some murals inside the Church. That would be a way of channeling Gonzo's creative talents in a positive direction.

And it would help heal a fractured community.

Dear Mickey:

Bless you for stepping in to help this handicapped talented man. Who in heaven's name on Roseville council has such a grudge against this man to spend all the city's resources to put an accomplished painter in jail? The Macomb Daily tells us of his offense with political signs in his window????? People as far away as Bloomington Hills told me they came to see his painting of Diana and shopped in Roseville and ate at a restaurant. All because of the "free advertising" Gonzo gets from those who oppose his paintings. How ridiculous to spend the City's money trying to put a handicapped painter out of business. I applaud the man for not going on welfare instead of practicing his painting that is his living. The public enjoys it according to all whom I come in contact with--- so who is nit picking on the council to "get this guy"??? For goodness sakes they need to get a life. Would Graffiti please them more? NOT THE VOTER'S, you always seem to go to bat for the "little guy" so have my thanks.

Best Regards,

C.H.

Roseville

Macomb Daily Editorial

"What does Roseville artist Edward Stross have in common with famous human rights leaders like Gandhi and the Rev. Martin Luther King Jr.? Not much, it turns out...

"He fled to a hospital when he discovered he was to be jailed for 30 days. Stross, who has made a name for himself over the years not so much for his art but with his defiance of the city zoning and sign ordinances, showed his true colors when he was unwilling to face the consequences of his crusade...

Stross is free to paint what he wants, when he wants and just about anywhere he wants, except on a single exterior wall of his commercial building on Gratiot. He even signed an agreement with city officials after a years-long feud over paintings on the wall in which he said he would not paint anything containing genitalia or words on the wall...

There is no absolute freedom of speech in this country, despite what the first amendment says. The courts throughout our nation's history have placed limitations on the absoluteness of that right. Stross wants it both ways. He wants to claim the freedom to paint what he wants on the wall, but he signed an agreement limiting some of his supposed rights, and now wants to renege on his word...

This is not a battle over freedom of expression. It's a simple city code dispute over the actions of one sore loser who doesn't want to abide by the same rules that his neighbors live by...."
(Philip Van Hulle, Macomb Daily, 20A, Feb. 27, 2005)

###

Dear Senator Switalski:

On a cold and dreary day, you have brought some sunshine into our home. It is a rare occasion, when a Senator or any other politician will speak up for the little guy and show a little compassion, this is very heartening.

I have met Mr. Stross a few times, he seems like a decent person, although misguided at times.

I have also met you a few times since your days on the council and thought that you were a bit odd at times. Maybe you have some artists' blood in you.

Senator Switalski, you have gained the respect of many people for your candid out front opinions. Tell it like it is philosophy. We love it.

Judge Santia has always been a fair and honest Judge. But we feel he caved in to the pressure the city council put on him. We truly hope this is not true. Maybe some good will come from this, and not have a bad ending.

Senator Switalski, on your bill to change campaign finance law, it's about time. Politicians have long felt that they were above the law, they help draft laws for everyone else. The fine you want to increase is too small. $5,000 will not send a message. It's a slap on the hand, make it $50,000 then watch the stampede!

Senator Switalski you are about to hit another home run. Enough accolades on your behalf....

Sincerely yours,

J. and M. K.

Roseville

P.S. Your Newsletter on the Trees was way out!

March 2005

That Sinking Feeling

"Hey Dad. You know that sinkhole?" wondered my son Liam, age 11. "What happened?"

"I'm glad you asked that question, son," I replied. "Lucky for you, I've toured that sinkhole four times."

"On August 27th, a portion of 15 Mile Road between Hayes and Schoenherr began to sink. Within a very short time, a 40-foot deep crater developed, causing the roadway above it to collapse, and nibbling perilously close to houses on the south side of 15 Mile. A second, smaller hole developed about 100 yards westward, maybe 25 feel deep. It was as if someone had pulled a plug and the earth was being sucked down a bottomless drain.

"All this was caused by a broken sewer pipe. Most people just flush wastewater down the drain and don't consider where it goes. Please allow me to describe what complex engineering is involved in fixing that pipe.

"Let's start with jurisdiction. The site is under the authority of the Detroit Water and Sewerage Department, or DWSD, and it has had lots of contractors-specialists from all over the country-working on it. They average about 60 people out there working 24/7 since the problem began. The City of Sterling Heights is the host of the site, and they protect the interests of the residents and coordinate with the DWSD. The state also has a regulatory function in terms of health and safety and the environment, and everyone works cooperatively to solve the problem."

"I ask you what time it is," complained Liam, "and you tell me how to build a watch."

"OK, smart guy. Here's what happened. Sixty feet below the surface of the ground, a huge concrete sewage pipe, 11 feet in diameter, ruptured. As raw sewage gushed from the broken pipe, it eroded the dirt surrounding the pipe. So began the great settling process that eventually created the giant sinkhole."

"So why didn't they just fill it back up?"

"Because all that would have sunk, too. It's like quicksand until you fix the source. First they had to stop the leak, and then stabilize the walls of the hole so it didn't get any bigger."

"I may regret asking this, but what did that involve?"

"They had to pound sheets of steel, like seawall, deep into the ground to keep the hole from getting any closer to people's houses. They had to drill into the ground with a spinning drill that shoots grout, a kind of liquid cement, at high pressure out the side as it goes down. That had the effect of creating cement pillars ten feet in diameter. They made about 18 of these, bisecting 15 Mile Road with about one foot between each column to stabilize the earth and allow limited migration of groundwater."

"That's all simply fascinating, Dad," said Liam. "Why don't they just dig down to the pipe and fix it so we can end this discussion."

"As much as you might like that, it is not that simple," I explained. "But you've posed a legitimate question. It's been four months now, and the repair has not been completed. Neighbors in the area have had to suffer the inconvenience of closed roads, noise, odor, and construction traffic. The City of Sterling Heights has worked hard to accommodate the residents, and city officials have had nothing but praise for the cooperation and professionalism of the DWSD, which is in charge of the repair."

"So what's taking so long?"

"Liam," I waxed, "to visit the site is to encounter an engineering project that rivals the construction of the Super Conducting Super Collider. I've already described the actions taken to stabilize the ground. Concurrently, the project managers acted to maintain sewage service-600 million gallons of sewage a day have to travel from Schoenherr to Hayes, but the pipe was broken. So they had to bypass the break. That means pumping all that sewage up to the surface, running it the better part of a mile alongside the break, before submerging it to the depths to link with the old pipe again.

"And that had to be done immediately, because the longer you wait, the more erosion and sinking you get. And if the broken pipe collapsed and completely stopped flowing, you would get a major sewage backup. And when sewage backs up there's only one place for it to go.

That would be a basement near you.

"So what's the big deal? Put in a bypass. We do it to heart patients all the time."

"Well, yes, we do. But it's a big deal when we do it there, too. And by the way, we better not just do one bypass. Because if that one fails, think one word again-basement."

"Wait a minute," Liam cried, alarmed for the first time. "My Nintendo's down there."

"Don't worry," I added. "That's why they did two bypass lines. They installed a 36- and a 24-inch pump, and they have replacements on hand, and two sets of pumps. The first sets ran on diesel and were loud and smelly. Since then, Edison ran power to the site, and the pumps are electric and quieter. But they kept the diesels, as a back up. And they run them for a short period once a day to make sure they don't freeze up. That wouldn't be much good in an emergency, would it?"

"Not when Godzilla Destroy all Monsters Melee is at risk."

"Right. Now as you can see, you need a lot of redundancies and backups in case of an emergency. And just in case everything went wrong, there was a final fail-safe option. If basements and video games were truly in jeopardy, the sewage could be diverted straight to the Red Run Drain a quarter mile away and treated with a large does of chlorine on the spot. All that is ready, too."

"I feel much better now," sighed Liam, turning toward the bathroom.

"Halt!" I shouted. "Hands high and step away from the toilet. Slowly."

He stepped gingerly away and glanced nervously at the plunger, standing menacingly in the corner.

"A funny thing happened as they dug down toward the pipe," I continued. "The whole area kept filling up with water. There's a huge retention pond just southeast of the site, and water was migrating into the hole from the surrounding high water table. So hydrologists had to dewater the entire area. They continue to pump groundwater out of the site on a daily basis. You'd be amazed at how clean it looks when it comes to the surface."

"Fascinating," he said, evenly. "So that's it, then? We're done?"

"Please remove your finger from that commode handle. We still have to fix the broken pipe, remember?"

"Oh yes," Liam recalled, scratching his head. "I knew there was a reason for all this."

"Now this is the good part," I warned him. "How would you like to climb down into that hole and fix that pipe?"

"Is this a trick question?"

"You just slide down the side on one of your boogie boards and slap a bandaid on the pipe, right."

"Sure, and have the sink hole suck me under and five tons of dirt cave in on top of me."

"Exactly. You wouldn't think it in this day and age, but 44 workers were killed in the U.S. by cave-ins last year. I'll bet most were down less than 60 feet, too. It is very dangerous work. That's why we have Occupational Safety and Health, or OSHA standards. So here's what they've done. I already told about pounding in the steel sheeting and the grouting to stabilize the area. To get at the broken pipe itself, they've had to drill a hole about three feet in diameter, perfectly straight down, and then lower a steel "I" beam 65-feet long into that hole. Then they pump cement down two tubes attached to the beam, so the beam sits in cement. And they fill the three-foot hole with cement so the beam is encased in cement."

"Wow."

"They do that 262 times in a rectangle around the area of the broken pipe. Then they scrape the cement from sections of the "I" beam and weld cross beams from side to side. It creates a reinforced cage for the men to work in as they uncover and replace the pipe.

"Double wow."

"They even lowered a steam shovel into the hole through the frame."

"Now can I go?"

'Wait," I told him. "There's more."

"I'm sure there is, Dad," Liam observed philosophically. "But I've been here wondering about something else. Did you know that the Nintendo 64 is so named because it was the first system to run on 64 frames of graphics?"

"No, I didn't, Liam," I replied. "What's a frame of graphics?"

January 2005

The Refuge of Scoundrels

Fifteen people now stand indicted in the largest public corruption case in the history of Macomb County. The Finance Director of East Detroit Schools is serving 13 months in prison after embezzling half a million dollars from the district. Two former East Detroit superintendents are under indictment, along with the Maintenance Director, and numerous contractors, including Bill Hudson, the General Contractor on the district's $27 million bond project.

Saddest of all, two school board members have already pled guilty, and a third is indicted, for taking money from Hudson. Thieves took advantage of the public's desire to support education and made the district a refuge for scoundrels. It is depressing to see elected officials betray their public trust, disgrace themselves, and cause such pain for their constituents and the children of their districts.

But the story of Hudson Construction and East Detroit Schools is not just a sad story of thievery and public corruption. It is also a heroic story about a dedicated public servant and the struggle of one individual against the system. Newly elected School Board member Veronica Klinefelt fought bravely against a dizzying array of entrenched forces. She brought them down by dint of her sheer determination and hard work. Hers is a David and Goliath story that is uniquely American.

I have no better friend than Veronica Klinefelt. She is a housewife, a mother of 4, daughter of an Army General and a friend who has stood by me like few others. She has gotten up with me at the crack of dawn for 4 years now to drop literature on a regular basis. I am proud to know her as my friend and ally.

After less than a year on the board Veronica began telling me of management and financial problems in the district. I was skeptical until June 1999 when she presented me with a smoking gun at her backyard picnic table.

The district ran a building trades program and Veronica believed the district was being overcharged. She demanded an accounting. Finance Director Scothorn did an audit and said Hudson Construction had been overpaid $80,000.

Veronica felt it had to be more. The district was paying full year tuition for students who only attended half a year. Scothorn did a second reconciliation, and claimed this time that the overpayment was only $48,000.

Veronica demanded a third audit, supplying her own figures and estimates, and this time Scothorn found a $383,000 overpayment. Klinefelt and Board ally Larry Burton demanded an independent audit and the smoking gun emerged. I broke the story in *The Insider (Vol. 4, No. 3, June 1999),* a month before the mainstream press picked up on the story. As I told the story then:

The auditor went to work and soon unearthed a letter, signed by both Scothorn and Hudson, admitting to a $681,000 overpayment, and promising that a payment plan would be established to collect the money. Accounting giant Plante & Moran, who had conducted the District's annual financial audit, had required the letter when they had discovered a major imbalance in East Detroit's accounts.

The letter was dated October, 1998.

That was a month before Klinefelt began asking for a reconciliation. How, one might be tempted to ask, could she have been given figures of $80,000, and then $48,000, and finally $383,000, when Hudson and the School had already agreed with the auditors and signed a letter that Hudson owed the District $681,000?

There can be no good answer to that question.

From that point forward I was a believer, and I marveled at Klinefelt's skill and resolution to bring the thieves to justice. I have known a lot of people in public life, and I could count on one hand the ones with the guts to do what she did. I don't think I could have done it.

The conspirators funded a recall effort against her, complete with full page ad in the *Eastsider* slamming her. Ousted superintendent Gardiner, currently under indictment, brought a defamation suit against her personally.

Veronica makes $2000 a year on the board. She had to hire a lawyer to defend herself with her own money. A weaker person would have given up. But she persevered and prevailed. Someday they will name a street in Eastpointe after her, and if not that, at least a car wash. That's the least they can do for someone who so effectively cleaned up the district.

Life in the House of the Lords

I spent 4 years in the House of Representatives.

And I loved every minute of it.

Serving in the legislature is like going off to college. You leave home and meet strangers from all over. And you learn a lot if you listen to the experts and ask a bunch of questions.

You get to know your colleagues. With term limits, there are only 3 classes: Freshmen, Sophomores and Seniors. In college, students ask, "What's your major?" Legislators ask, "What committees are you on?"

I feel lucky every day I walk into the Capitol. Heroic architecture inspires you to value and respect the grandeur of our democratic institutions. You try hard to be worthy.

If the House is college, the Senate is definitely Graduate School. I loved the House for its raucous sessions, irreverent food fights, its frequent all-nighters, and its outlandish characters. It was barely organized chaos.

The Senate is quite different.

For one thing, it's far more disciplined and professional. The Senate has 38 members compared to 110 in the House. Its members are generally more experienced. There are 11 house members in their 20s, including four 22-year olds. In contrast, almost all of the Senators were representatives and also have experience in local government. Age brings a certain maturity and *gravitas* to the job.

The Senate is far more organized. When I was in the House, check in time was 2 pm for the start of session. But we *never* started at two. Roll Call for attendance would begin at two, but then would drag on and on. People would straggle in late, and soon people stopped coming at two, because we never started at two. So people started coming at 2:15. Before you know it, we were starting at 2:30.

In the Senate, the gavel comes down every day at 10 am sharp. You have 1 minute to check in, and the clock is running. You also have one minute to vote. In the House, leadership used to keep the voting board open for hours, especially when the Speaker of the House was short of votes to pass a bill and needed to change a few representatives' minds. Sometimes members would *clear the board* and end a vote if it wasn't coming out the way they wanted.

Not in the Senate.

No *clearing the board* once a vote starts. Votes are tallied after exactly one minute. No fast gavel in the Senate. No being ignored by the presiding officer. And if anyone wants a recorded vote, just ask and you get a record roll call vote.

These rules ensure respect for the institution, members' time, and the integrity of the process.

I like that

No long interminable speeches, either. In the House people would drone on for what seemed like hours, and then ask to be recognized to speak again. In the Senate, you get 5 minutes. When the clock runs out, the gavel comes down and you are done. If you can't make your point in 5 minutes, you need an editor.

Plus, we actually *listen* to one another. If you ever watch the House on TV, we almost never listened to one another's speeches. In the Senate, it is actually quiet and most Senators value the debate, by listening, even if they are not speaking.

How refreshing.

I chaired the Democratic Caucus meetings, which was like herding cats. The meetings would go on for hours. After two hours of our 52 members sharing their opinions on some issue, some of them several times, we would ask members to conclude the debate. But members would insist on having their say.

"Everything that could possibly be said has already been said," I noted on more than one occasion. *"But not by everybody."*

And so the debate would continue.

Thankfully, we are not so self-indulgent in the Senate.

Still, for all its faults, I wouldn't trade my 4 years in the House for anything.

But with all due respect, *the Senate Rules.*

June 2003

The New Legislature

As required by the Michigan Constitution, we began the 93rd session of the Michigan Legislature at noon Wednesday, January 12th. The two-year session begins with Michigan still suffering economically, and with the state struggling with its 4th straight year of significant financial problems.

The Michigan House of Representatives welcomed 39 new freshman members. They join 51 members who now have two years of experience. The most senior members, who have four years of experience, only number 20.

Think about that. Out of a chamber of 110 members, 90 of them have two years of experience or less. That includes the new House Speaker, who will have to learn quickly how to assimilate and lead the members.

Four years ago, during my second term in the House, I was elected Chairman of the Democratic Caucus. That was a difficult job, and we only had 52 members. My job was likened to "herding cats."

Members are each elected by their own constituents, so leaders really are the "first among equals." Independent representatives don't like being told what to do, where to go, or how to vote. Sometimes they do the opposite of what you want them to do, just to show you that you aren't their boss. I remember just trying to enforce some order with the gavel during one caucus, and a colleague berated me, calling me a tyrant and a dictator.

So I wish the new Speaker, and all the leaders in both chambers, the best of luck in the New Year.

Michigan has had term limits for six years now, and although most people that work in or with government profess to hate the limits, polls show consistent support among the general public for the practice. In fact, whenever an amendment has been on the ballot in any state to eliminate or extend the length of term limits, the voters have overwhelmingly rejected it. People like term limits and they don't want to change them.

At the end of each term, speculation rises about the legislature attempting to change the law, but nothing has happened so far. Term limits are like the weather. Everybody likes to talk about it, but nobody does anything about it.

236

Every time politicians start talking about changing the term limit law, the pro-term limit people get all excited and start threatening anyone who dares to question the law. I got a package in the mail from some term limit group, suggesting I'd better sign a pledge, promising that I won't touch the term limit law, if I know what's good for me.

I don't sign pledges, even though I actually like term limits. I probably would never have got to Lansing if it weren't for the term limit law. I do think that politicians brought the term limit law on themselves by giving incumbents advantages like franking privileges and manipulating redistricting to create safe seats for both parties.

But I also think that six years in the Michigan House of Representatives is too short. I think it should be extended to eight years for House members, and everything else left as it is. That would mean a consistent 8-year limit for House of Representatives, Senators, Governors, Secretaries of State and Attorney Generals. Just adding two years to the House would mean a world of difference in terms of the experience and stability of the Chamber, and it wouldn't really violate the spirit of term limits. I tried to explain this to the people who sent me the pledge, but their minds don't appear to be open to a discussion of the merits of my proposal.

They are in good company. Most of the people who want to extend term limits aren't interested in my proposal either. Why do all that work for a measly two-year extension? They want something like 12 years for both chambers, which moves us back to the career politicians that term limits was precisely designed to eliminate.

So it's clear to me that there is no realistic prospect of changing the term limit law, even in the moderate way that I have suggested. So we have to make the best of it.

Right now the Senate is the most senior chamber, and it shows. The leadership team has been in Lansing for 20 years or more. The rest of the Senators have been together for six years, so they've been able to develop good relationships and trust with colleagues on both sides of the aisle. That means a lot when you are trying to pass controversial legislation.

As a consequence, most of the deals between the Governor and the Legislature have been made in the Senate the last two years, with the House, sometimes reluctantly, joining along. Having a little extra influence in making the tough decisions for our state has made the job especially enjoyable the last two years.

I look forward to the chance to help steer Michigan to better times in 2005.

January 2005

Poetry

Spreading the Holiday Cheer, Legislative Style

Has the snow and bitter cold got you down in the pits? Is dodging salt trucks and snow banks keeping you from enjoying your morning commute? Is shopping for your loved ones adding undue stress and agitation?

Take stock that, well, you are not the only one. There are millions facing a similar fate, including myself. The Holidays are upon us and help is on the way. I would like to spread some holiday cheer with you, Mickey Switalski-style.

Legislators often make statements before the legislative body but during the last days of session before the Christmas break, there is a mad scramble to get things done before everyone leaves to go out of town. It is common for the Legislature to pull some long days and sometimes even late nights in an effort to pass numerous pieces of legislation.

Debate is intense, courtesy goes out the window, and everyone is restless and wants to go home. So over the years, I have made some speeches on the floor, in an attempt to instill some bipartisan Holiday spirit among my slightly perturbed legislative colleagues. Here is a sampling, as quoted from the Senate Journal:

Xmas Statement, 2003

"After some prodding by some colleagues and friends, I am going to repeat some remarks I made some years ago in another chamber, recalling some ghosts of Christmas Past. So please indulge me by closing your eyes, and listen as I relate the astounding events on the last day of session long, long ago."

T'was the night before recess
In the Michigan House.
All the members were restless
When Rep. Hale spied a mouse.

A wee sleekit, and cow' rin',
And tim' rous beastie
Put a panic into
Irma Clark's comely breastie.

He scampered across the desks
into a crack.
Derrick Hale scampered faster
To the arms of Kilpa'ck.

Rocky pounded the rostrum
To call us to order.
Still some bills to be passed
And our time had grown shorter.

Just 10 minutes left
To the end of the session.
Plus the Speaker's remarks
An important digression.

Two bills hung in the balance
My favorites, too.
One was for me
And the other one, you.

That's the way it is done
If you want some success.
Especially when
Your side numbers the less.

Just 10 minutes left.
Would Chuck be verbose?
If we go beyond midnight,
My bill's comatose.

The adoption tax credit
Would die at midnight.
The end of the session
Kills all bills with spite.

But then time stood still
By divine intervention.
Or maybe a button
Under Randall's attention.

The Speaker was eloquent.
The clock made no move.
It's still 'leven fifty
With 12 bills to approve.

My bill came to the floor
And was passed in a rout.
Who says that two Freshmen
Don't have any clout?

The session then ended
Two minutes to spare.
How be it 1:30
When I walked out of there?

I preferred the strange mystery
When the truth reached my ears.
Next day's clock inspection
Found a mouse in the gears.

Merry Christmas to all."

Xmas Address, 2004

"I rise to offer you all a song in the spirit of Christmas. Besides, it's cheaper than sending out cards. I ask your forgiveness in advance, with further apologies to the late great Senate crooner, George Hart."

I Saw Kenny Kissing Jenny G

I saw Kenny kissing Jenny G
Underneath the Cap'tol Dome last night.
Bob didn't see us sneak
Out the Caucus room to peek.
Thought Shirley'd locked us in Approps to cut the budgets deep.

Some Dems were hopeful Jenny'd right all wrongs.
Six years in minority gets old.
Ken's colleagues on the right
Wanted him to pick a fight.
But fightin's only fun when there's some kissin' to be done.

Elephants and Donkeys often clash.
It is just the nature of the beasts.
House members on the floor
Can't conceive that less is more.
The Senate session's done before the House comes in the door.

Now we've been broke a good 4 years or so.
Can't hit people with a tax hike now.
So smokers took some shots,
And the gamblers on the slots,
But Early County Mill Collection ain't a tax increase.

So when you go home to your family now
Thank our leaders for the job they've done.
Oh, what a laugh it would have been

Had Perricone only seen
Kenny kissing Jenny G last night."

At the request of the author, all audio copies of this presentation were destroyed with "extreme prejudice."

Xmas Message, 2005

"I just wanted to take this opportunity to wish everyone a Merry Christmas and Happy Holidays. Many of you have begged me, implored me, not to sing. I respect that and I will honor your wishes. But I thought I would share a wee limerick with you:

A fine looking Gov'nor named Jenny
Had me over her house times a-plenty.
She gave me a kiss
'Twas the ultimate bliss.
If my wife learns, I'll never get any.

I give you now Cameron Brown
Looks a debonair man-about-town.
He's ever fine spoken,
Enjoys Funk Brothers smokin'
And he seeks the Republican crown.

Warren's telecom expert is Dennis,
Although Patterson thought him a menace.
He was briefly befuddled
And his driving was scuttled
By an ill-advised trip to the dentist.

Now with Martha you have my assurance
That a statement you'll hear on insurance.
Might there be a rate cut?
No consensus now, but
The election may bring us concurrence.

The Approps chair is known as Good Shirley,
Though her rulings can sometimes be squirrelly.
When targets are set,
It's a pretty good bet
That she's got Prusi tight by the curlies.

Bob Emerson hails from Flint,

A city that's virtually skint.
He wont take campaign chair.
And when pressed, stamps and swears
Barking, "Grow up!" We won't take the hint.

Leader Sikkema hails from Grandville
So hard-headed they call him The Anvil.
But when he makes a deal,
He won't dither or squeal
Like that back-sliding House-leading man will.

But we can't be too hard on DeRoche,
For to do so would be very gauche.
It's a real bad idearia
I'll be sent to Siberia.
My new colleagues will call me Milosch.

I'll quit now 'cause I think I'm ahead.
If I don't stop, I may wind up dead.
It's been great being here
And we'll see you next year.
Merry Christmas it's off to my bed."

Xmas Message, 2006

This is a bittersweet day, sine die approaches, and the two-year session of the 93rd Legislature is adjourning and the four-year term of every senator in these chambers is expiring. The last of the old guard, the grizzled legislators prior to term limits and who are the repository of the great traditions of this institution, are leaving us, perhaps to never return, and taking with them a collection of knowledge and experience that is as invaluable as it is irreplaceable.

I find that in these final poignant hours, as the last of our veteran colleagues depart, that my soul is moved to sing. Allow me to present the Caucettes who have agreed to appear with me and it was a very difficult task assembling the Caucettes. I asked a number of people. The last time I was turned down this much was my high school prom. So I beg your indulgence for a medley I call, "Next time send me the box of Clementines."

Next Time Send Me a Box of Clementines

Thanks for the memories
I knelt at Kenny's desk
To hear his new request.
And if I give my vote I hope
The Dems won't cut my throat
For some measly crumb.

Negotiations
Ken hammers out a deal.
He'd squeeze until I'd squeal.
He sold me sleeves
From off his vest
And told me it's a steal.
Protesting, he'd say:

"Let's close this deal now.
This bargain is a keeper.
My commitment's never deeper.
But wait a sec,
So I can check
If Burton sells out cheaper."

And POOF! goes the deal.

So Thank Ken for give and take
Of buying what we bid
And some deals we never did.
We used some tricks
To try and fix
Mistakes that can't be hid.
So Thanks and Goodbye.

Dems call Bob's name
But he's not there.
Term Limits blame
For being unfair.
He kept the caucus room bagels fresh
Carmel-Pecan Snack.
He taught us policy
Cuz we don't know Jack.

Don't you know we can't fake it
We're not qualified
We're not gonna ma-a-ake it,
Looks like Michigan's fri-i-i-ied.

Our constituents won't sleep at night
Once Bob's gone home.
Let's speed dial Emerson
And Call Bob's name.

Rockin' around the Capitol
There's the Leland trailer hitch.
Burton's bundlin' up his stuff
His wife's helping him make the switch.
You had best be careful
If you visit late at night.
If the Leland trailer's rockin'
Just be sure you don't go knockin'.

Down in the basement Hammerstrom
Runs the floor with lots of pep.
Cropsey's tall but not like Bev

When she stands up on her step.
She alone ran bills
That her own leader
Didn't like.
Hammerstrom's a splendid teacher
Fearless, feisty, spark plug leader.

I Gotchka go, it's getting late
Can't skip Michael in the back.
Presided over Higher Ed
Where he put the schools on track.
Complex tiers he explained
In Committee, and we saw
When he finished up his magic
All the money went to Saginaw.

Shirley J. appropriates
She's a tough old bird you know.
If you talk too much on bills
She will tell you where to go.
Cutting budgets, raisin' bucks
Tryin' to keep the wolf at bay.
Piggy bank up on her desk
It's the new old-fashioned way.

More? We did prepare an encore just in case. Caucettes,
are you ready?

Listen, Do Wah Do.
Do you want to know a secret: Do Wah Do.
Cameron Brown is soon to wed.
Oh, oh, oh, closer.
Do Wah Do
Let me whisper in your ear. Do Wah Do.
Words that Cameron's bound to hear.
"Honey, you forgot to take out the trash."
Woo, Woo, Woo
"Honey, can you pick up a gallon of milk?"
Woo, woo, woo.
"Cameron, you left the toilet seat up again."
                    Woo, Woo, Woo.

Xmas Message, 2007

Traditionally, on the last day of session, I share with my legislative colleagues wishes of a Happy Holiday season with a reflection on the year gone by. Over the years, this has taken on various forms, from poems to songs. In the holiday spirit, I wish to share with you this year's installment. I hope you enjoy and have a safe and wonderful Holiday season and New Year.

To my Legislative Colleagues: Our year together is ending. Please accept this humble poem as my way of wishing you Happy Holidays. It's much easier than sending you all Christmas Cards.

I appreciate the good taste of many who begged me, implored me, not to sing. To those of you that urged instead, a medley from the Caucquettes: I join you in extending an invitation to those charming and melodious performers.

But now let me turn to a review of *My Favorite Year*. Colleagues, we have been *Present at the Creation*. For decades to come, 2007 will be the focus of fiscal debate. Accordingly, nothing less than the language of Homeric Epic will suffice to tell the tale of this *Miraculous Year*.

Annus Mirabilis
A Fiscal Odyssey

Sing, Goddess, the Wrath of Constituencies displeased,

As Solons took budgets in both hands and squeezed.

Then, weary with cuts, dropped the red budget axe

And seized its hated rival, the increase in tax.

Heroes searched for a cure to the Plague economic

Hit on Revenue, Cuts and Reforms as the tonic--

That many brave Pols to the Fate of Recalls sent

While their bodies by Perks the Pig were rent.

Say then, What Cause first locked the parties in strife?

Some say it was term limits that shortened our life.

Or exuberant tax cuts. Or government waste.

Whatever it was, we Chronic Deficits faced.

Granholm threw down the Gauntlet at her State of the State.

Said she "Sales Tax on Services will be Structurally Great."

The blown away 'Crats cast their votes for fair Jenny
Even Fiscal Conservatives, like two-penny Denny.
But with just sixteen votes, it was never enough.
Lawmakers decided to chew on this stuff.
Insurmountable problems, an abundance of critics.
Tempting solutions that hid pitfalls and gimmicks.
Like Damocles' Sword, one hung over our head.
SBT Abolition, by Brooks Patterson led.
No replacement in sight, and the deadline grew near.
Two billion buck shortfall, and collapse appeared clear.
'Fore we even got started, a Red Torrent intervened
A billion plus bucks from '07 to be weaned.
"No tax increase," we vowed, with a laser-like focus,
'stead used mirrors, and smoke, and slick Hocus Pocus.
Poof! The budget was balanced. Then how could it jive
That '08 rouged up by a bill seven-five?
One-time fixes were culprits, there was now no excuse.
So we solemnly vowed to abolish their use.
First Surprise of the Summer, a quick compromise struck.
And a new MBT deal emerged from the muck.
Rivals Cassis and Bieda, after pulling out hair
Got us Revenue Neutral, with six months to spare.
A bi-partisan deal, inspiring to all
Gave us hope as we turned to the '08 shortfall.
There was lots of bad feeling, and loads of mistrust
Angry words to the Press in which rivals were cussed.
Under cover of darkness, 'neath the Capitol Dome,
A cabal met in secret, in a Senator's home.
Resurrected the Service Tax, which six worked to tailor
A concept designed by Valde the Impaler.
But nobody liked it, so t'was fast set aside
'Cuz the House of Reps promised to deliver a tide--
Of votes for the Income Tax, but all they could muster
Was a lot of false starts, and a big heap of bluster.
The Summer boiled on, amid heightening fears

That the State would establish a Sin Tax on Beers.
Then came the three nights the House Board remained open.
Tho' Dillon had promised 4.6, he was jokin'.
You need five six for four six but they always were short.
So late Sunday Morning Andy had to abort.
Wags crowed, "Dill ain't up to fillin' his roles."
Next week he closed five hundred mill in loopholes.
The House had moved Revenue. But Bishop was cool.
He'd won eight hundred million, in cuts, through his Rule.
We fought, push-pull, parry-thrust, shot and rebound
As we staggered, unwilling, to a Lansing Shutdown.
The Shutdown would start on October the 1st.
The way we were battlin', the World thought the worst.
Would we all go down, our accomplishments: none
A bunch of thick Morons who couldn't git 'r done?
Looking back now, Hindsight makes you wise.
We all had to know it would take Compromise.
Needed Tax and Reform, and we had to have Cuts
Slashed four thirty-three million, no ifs, ands, or buts.
Then took up Reforms, the vote would be tight.
When you're cutting bennies, it's always a fight.
Health Care and Pensions for teachers were trimmed
Future prospects for Me, Buzz and Schauer were dimmed.
My Republican colleagues, to their Word remained true.
In return for Reforms, now the Revenue grew.
Birkholz, Van Woerkom, Garcia and George
Jel'nek and Kuipers took the heat of the Forge.
The end was a blur, in those hours past midnight.
I know, in my heart, that we did, what was right.
It got a bit crazy when we put up IE.
I wish I'd just gone to the back, for a . . . tea.
Month later, the last few departments were done.
Traded Service for Surcharge, still under the gun!
But together we posted the ultimate score:
A bi-partisan tax vote of 34-4.

I'll leave it to others to explain the great lessons
Of Wisdom emerging from those late-night sessions.
But know this: Center aisle is where deals get done.
And being part of solutions is a whole lot of fun.
Merry X-mas to All

December 2007

Christmas Poem, 2008

Senator Switalski's statement is as follows (as quoted in the Senate Journal, December 19, 2008):

"Because I am both an environmentally-conscious tree saver, plus my office budget has been cut, I am wishing you Happy Holidays today with a poem, in lieu of sending you all Christmas cards. I want to apologize to my staff, who begged to hear my message yesterday, but as with Santa and the poem, there is more fun in the anticipation than in the thing itself. Besides, my Christmas message is best delivered late at night to fatigued, bored, and nearly comatose legislators who are thoroughly starved for entertainment.

Only in this environment do my poetic talents flourish. So if you promise not to throw any shoes at me, without further ado, I give you now "A Christmas Carol":

Once, upon a midnight dreary,
Pondering bills and email queries,
And many a quaint and curious 'mendment to forgotten law.
Sat in session, nearly napping
Drool came out, like pine tree sapping.
Suddenly there came a tapping, gently rapping, upon the Senate Chamber Door.
'Twas Justice Taylor woke me
Whispered, "Wake! But please don't quote me."
Once Supreme, his dusty robes were tattered now and tore.
His warning got me thinking
Chamber cameras are unblinking
Seeking shots of snoring Solons on the Senate Chamber floor.
"Come with me," rose Taylor, beckoning.
"Sessions Past are due a reckoning.
I will show you things you never knew, and never saw before."
We flew up above the ceiling
To the catwalk, sent mice squealing
And looked down upon the Grandeur of the Upper Chamber Floor.
Through mists I saw a Session Past,
A long debate and tax vote cast,
That ended Chronic Deficits, while caring for the Poor.
Pat, Tom, Gere, and Jelinek

Valde 'n Wayne stuck out their neck.
Went on the Board for Revenues and made The Chamber Sore.
The Dems had to offend their own,
Who normally they'd throw a Bone,
And make Reforms to Bennies that shook teachers to the core.
Buzz and Mark and just one other
Now loved only by their mother
"Enough!" barked Taylor. "Lose that grin. I've heard this all
before."
"Your Legacy today's in doubt.
The Big 3 now are in a rout."
And the Ghost of Session Present breathed a Freeze upon the
floor.
EO cut one-forty million
2010 could hit a billion
And Recession may the Deficits of Sessions Past Restore.
"Not that!" I cried.
"Those figures lied!
Could Jan's Estimating Conference please send Wolfie from the
Door?"
Now the ghost of Sessions Future
Cut our budgets like a Butcher.
We're so desperate now, even Sacred Cows, we're willing to
Explore.
The Shade's vision of the Future
Like a hemorrhage, needs a suture.
Or a tourniquet to staunch the flow of jobs gone out the door.
Unemployment's double digit
Causes budget hawks to fidget
Should we raise Debt, creating Work, and make employment
Soar?
We've 2 years of Future Sessions
Wrack our brains to end Recessions
And Faith and Hope and Confidence and Zest for Life Restore.
Let's do it all together
Now enjoy the Christmas weather.
'Cause when Janus comes we cannot Sleep no More.

So Merry Christmas, everyone."

January 2009

The Freshmen 64, 2010

When we were 64
New Freshmen in the House
It was a very good year for Supplemental spending 'ppropriation Bills.
Funds stacked up high in mammoth hills
Spending was tops among our skills
We Freshmen 64.

But in our second term,
It wasn't such a good year.
The dot.com bubble fin'lly burst and Enron made things worse
A deficit appeared.
Our Budget now looked weird
To one-time fixes we were geared.
During our second term.

Into the Senate Sworn
It was a very good year.
It was a very good year for focusing debate with 5 minute rules
Suffer no Filibuster Fools
Or "Clear the Board" Duels
With Upper Chamber Rules.

Now it's our Final Senate Days
We've had some very good years
We've shared a laugh and a tear
We've fought and we've jeered a Common Enemy we've Feared.
So one last time while we're still here
Quick let's Adjourn, with the House here
Let's make them work while we drink beer.

So if I see you again
While selling pencils in the street.
Just pull your Limo to the side
I'll polish off your feet 'n wash the windows of your Ride.
You'll wink and let me slide
Toss me a piece of chicken fried
We're friends until we've died
We Freshmen 64.

Senate's Over (You Still Want It?)

And so it's Sine Die
And what have you done?
Our last session is over
And a new one soon begun.
All your unpassed Legislation
Is buried in dust
Dreams of World Domination
Are a Total Bust.

Did you accomplish your mission?
A skillful Lawmaker does.
"Well, I tried to tweak something
but I forgot what it was."

Senate's over
You still want it?
Lame Duck Quacker
Bunch of Slackers

So clean out your desk now
And ask Snyder for work

Hope he gives you a good one
If you aint been a jerk.
So say bye to your staffers
Tell them no one's to blame
But don't bother the Lobby
They've all forgotten your name.

Terms are over
No one wants us
No enjoyment
Unemployment.

So go back to your District
So long absent from Home
All you meet now are strangers
Least you got this cool poem.

Merry Christmas Everybody!

Verses on the Death of Senator Switalski

We 64 Freshmen, Term Limits' First Class
Came to Lansing determined, to take names and kick. . . *back*.
I was one among many, and to prominence rose
Caucus Chair in the House, Senate *Vice* of Appro's.

Quite full of myself, when the Holidays came
Read poems and sang songs, though most were quite lame.
But now the hour has come, when I must depart
So in *this* my last *message*, let me speak from the Heart.

It's been a great run, 12 years under the Dome
With term limits arrival, its now time to go home.
Did I make the place better, with my hard work and wit?
Or was I *less effective*, than a *bucket of spit?*

I'm the champion bill sponsor, and had lots of PA's.
I will *now* use my talents, getting people BA's.
Allow me to reflect, on the place when I'm gone
Will great scholars research me, o'er my legacy fawn?

Why sure that could happen, but in the meantime
My status has changed, I'm a cut below slime.
When I came *late* for meetings, back *then* everything stopped.
People jumped up to greet me, placing me at the top.

But *now* if I come late, they've locked up the door
If I force my way in, they say "Sit on the floor!"
"Are you sure you're invited? Let me check the guest list.
There's space in the o-flow, or far back in the dist'."

When I walk in my office, my staff gives not a toss
Their allegiance *long transferred,* to their incoming boss.
"But I brought you some donuts," they're unmoved by my bribe.
"Where's that Letter of Rec, that you promised to scribe?"

Was it so long ago, that they catered my whims?
Expounded my virtues, to my praises sang hymns?
I beg of my intern, "Going to *Beaners* by chance?"
"You'll get nothing from me, 'less you pay in advance."

"Here's a fiver," I say, "Get a latte that's frothered."
"You'd best get it yourself 'cuz I canny be bothered."
So I go down myself, but never before
I've got every aide's order, plus the temp from Mancorps.

It's worse in the Lobby, as I sift thru the crowd
I'm a ghost, eyes go thru me, so I keep my head bowed.
Wait! Yellow slip has my name, between votes I can come!
But Kris Kraft only wants it, to wrap up her chewed gum.

I still get some emails, and constituent visits
I hear their long stories, and explain my term limits.
The next thing I know, they've leapt up from the table
And they're beating a path down the hall to N. Vrable.

The week after I'm gone, a school comes for a tour
Stephanie takes them around, but the Chamber's secured.
A Student steps forward, and says he wants to hear
Her recount the exploits of my Senate career.

"Swisstalski? You say? He does not ring a bell.
Did he sweep up the floors? Or old magazines sell?
He never was one of the famous anointed.
Perhaps he was to Bean Commission appointed."

My gal pals meet for breakfast, District Judge Laura Baird
Deb Cherry 'n Kat Wilbur, who all for me cared.
"Have you heard from Switalski? The old fool is a wreck.
We should find some *new* sap, who will pick up the check."

"Did I see some sad letter, from him belly-achin'"
I forget what it was, can you please pass the bacon?"
"I like having a man at our meals *if he's cooking.*
Forget about Mickey. Find some guy better-looking."

"We can trade in Switalski. With Switalski replace.
Get Rep Jon Switalski, whom the women all chase.
Or his big brother Mark, the Circuit Court judge.
I'd even settle for Matt. Have you tasted the Fudge?"

So my friends toss me over. But it's far worse at home
Than it ever was under the Capitol Dome.
"Did you take out the garbage? I've now told you three times.
Just Quit wasting your time with those moronic rhymes."

The indignities mount, so I dream of my end
I see through the mists, how my last hour is penned.
Outside dropping *Insiders*, a cold day in the 'ville,
As I get near the porch, I trip on an ant hill.

Fall head-first into stone steps, which I hit on the side
After stars, all goes black, and I've quietly died.
Wife Roma, son Liam give brief muffled sighs
then listen while others, my career eulogize.

There's a peck of detractors, who detail my warts
And my failure to trim excess robes from the Courts.
"A notorious skinflint. Why'd he get on Approps?
The Leaders back then must have really been dopes."

"He ran up big debts, left us all unemployed.
I won't shed any tears, now that he's been destroyed.
Never fixed our economy, or repaired the Big Three
When I think of useless, I spell Switalski."

A few bear my Defense, as best as they can
Since they lack ammunition, they describe my élan.
"He did lots of things, you wags fail to surmise
On him we depended, to wear Tartan Ties."

So Damned by faint praise, I don't know what is worse
Turns out my legacy's more of a curse.
So I wish you all well, as we head for our Rest
The most we can say, is we gave it our Best.

About the Author

Michael Norbert Switalski was born in Hamtramck, Michigan on January 11, 1955. He attended Sacred Heart School before graduating from Roseville High School in 1973, when he was voted *Class Wit*. He spent the rest of his life trying to draw the vital distinction between *wit* and *class clown*. He graduated from Louisiana State University in 1977 with a BA in Classical Languages and in 1981 earned an MA in History. His career as a professional student ended in 1982 with an M. Litt. in Politics, ABD from the University of Aberdeen in Scotland.

In the early 80's, he eked out a living as Sports Editor for the *Utica Advisor* and C&G Newspapers, and was a frequent contributor to the *Detroit Free Press* and stringer for Ernest Hemingway's old paper, the *Kansas City Star*. His adventures as a newspaper baron reached full fruition when he began publishing *The Insider* in 1996.

Mickey served as the Head of Labor Relations at the Detroit Arsenal Tank Plant during a decade of toil for General Dynamics from 1985-93. His political career began with his elevation to the Roseville City Council in 1989. He was elected Macomb County Commissioner in 1992 and Michigan State Representative in 1998. In 2002, Mickey was elected to the Michigan Senate, rising to minority vice chair of the Appropriations Committee. He left the Legislature in 2011 after an unsuccessful run for Congress, and is now an instructor in History and Politics at Macomb Community College and Baker College.

He has coached championship soccer teams, first as skipper of the Roseville Rowdies in the mid—80's, and then at the helm of the Roseville Yellowsnakes at the turn of the millennium, thanks largely to the skills of players like Sebastian Switalski and Liam Heaney Switalski. His coaching career reached its apex when he took over a 2-11 St. Angela grade school basketball team in 2005 and won successive CYO league titles, going 10-0 in 2005/6.

Mickey married Roma Heaney in Glasgow, Scotland in 1985, and the pair was blessed with a son, Liam, in 1993. After successfully spiriting his mother Nancy away from his brother in 2008, he achieved domestic bliss. The three generations all live happily together in Roseville, Michigan.